About M

How would I describe Smiler? Tough, leads by example, focused, resilient – but it keeps coming back to him being 'just a good bloke'. I remember how hard we trained in the 2008 Six Nations campaign and Matthew was inspiring in the way he pushed himself and led from the front.

It was no surprise that Matthew faced the challenge of overcoming testicular cancer in 2013 with the same determination and resolve that he has displayed throughout his rugby career, coming back to play again for Wales in 2014.

WARREN GATLAND, HEAD COACH, WALES

Matthew is one of the fiercest and most determined players I have ever played with. One of the few players you would want in your team when things aren't going to plan. Tough and uncompromising. A fantastic leader who I've learnt so much from, and he must surely be one of Wales' greatest hookers.

SAM WARBURTON,
WALES AND THE BRITISH AND IRISH LIONS

A player who leads from the front, a physical ball carrier – he motivated players on the pitch. When you took the field with Smiler, you knew he would not take a backward step.

STEPHEN JONES,
WALES AND THE BRITISH AND IRISH LIONS

I knew of him as a player before I played against him, and when I did play against him I realised how good he was. He was one of the new breed of hookers, not just good at the set piece, but a strong ball carrier as well and good around the field in most facets of play.

When we were in the Welsh squad together, after many team runs we would share a coffee, with me often buying – Matthew does not like to part with his money too often.

Matthew would go on to be my captain for Wales and he was a fine captain, leading by example.

During many games against him when he carried the ball with his forearm protected by his forearm pad, often he would contact some part of my upper body, and I would then see him running away with a smile on his face, which we would have a laugh and a joke about next time we met up.

As is well known, Matthew has overcome adversary in his life, and the way he has bounced back and is still playing speaks volumes about the man.

ALUN WYN JONES,
WALES AND THE BRITISH AND IRISH LIONS

It's a pleasure to say a few words in Matthew's book.

I have known Matthew for over 20 years and have battled with and against him on the rugby field, from playing against him in our school days to playing alongside him for Wales and the Lions.

He has been on an incredible journey and I'm sure this book will reflect the magnitude of his achievements on the field and the toughness and spirit he has shown off it in overcoming every obstacle thrown in his way.

We are still close friends and enjoy each other's company at the Cardiff Blues. I wish him every success with the book and look forward to a few controversial paragraphs and stories from over the years!!

GETHIN JENKINS,
WALES AND THE BRITISH AND IRISH LIONS

MATTHEW REES

REASONS 2 SMILE

MATTHEW
REES

REASONS 2 SMILE

MY BATTLES ON AND OFF THE RUGBY FIELD

WITH CRAIG MUNCEY

First impression: 2018

© Copyright Matthew Rees, Craig Muncey
and Y Lolfa Cyf., 2018

The publishers wish to acknowledge the support of
Cyngor Llyfrau Cymru

Cover photograph: Ben Evans from Huw Evans Agency
Cover design: Y Lolfa

ISBN: 978 1 78461 593 2

Published and printed in Wales
on paper from well-maintained forests by
Y Lolfa Cyf., Talybont, Ceredigion SY24 5HE
website www.ylolfa.com
e-mail ylolfa@ylolfa.com
tel 01970 832 304
fax 832 782

Contents

Acknowledgements

I'D LIKE TO thank all my friends both within rugby and outside of the sport for all their support over the years. I'd also like to thank the Welsh Books Council and Y Lolfa for giving me the opportunity to tell my story, and to Huw and Ben Evans for permission to use photos for this book.

Thank you to all Velindre staff for their unbelievable care through my battle with cancer. Without them I wouldn't be here and this book wouldn't have been written.

Thank you to Jon Williams of PAS Nutrition for providing the supplements which have kept me on the rugby pitch. Heartfelt thanks to all my coaches for their support and developing me as a player. Thanks also to the medical staff at all my clubs and internationally for keeping this body going.

A special thanks to Warren Gatland for his kind words in the foreword for the book, and also for playing such a big part in my rugby career.

Final thanks to all of my family, and in particular Becky and Brooke for always being there and keeping me grounded.

Matthew Rees
October 2018

Foreword

'How would I describe Smiler?' was my first thought when I was asked to write the foreword for his book. The following came to mind – tough, leads by example, focused, resilient and more, but in Matthew's case it kept coming back to him being 'just a good bloke'.

Arriving in Wales at the end of 2007 in time for the 2008 Six Nations, I was tasked with putting some respect back into the Welsh jersey after the disappointing exit from the 2007 Rugby World Cup.

We picked the team for that first game against England, a nation we hadn't beaten at Twickenham for 20 years! Everyone was amazed that we named 13 Ospreys. Matthew came off the bench for the last 22 minutes, making a significant contribution as we came from behind and closed out the game. We broke the drought and went on to win a well-deserved Grand Slam.

I remember how hard we trained in that Six Nations campaign and Matthew was inspiring in the way he pushed himself and led from the front in a great battle for the No. 2 spot with Huw Bennett.

In 2009 I know what a huge thrill it was for Matthew to be selected for the British and Irish Lions tour of South Africa. Gethin Jenkins, Matthew Rees and Adam Jones were all selected to start in the second Test in Pretoria. Their impact in this match was obvious and I still regret that we didn't use this combination in the first Test.

It was in recognition of Matthew's leadership qualities that he was named as Captain for the 2011 Six Nations campaign and, conversely, a huge disappointment that he couldn't attend the Rugby World Cup in New Zealand the same year due to a neck injury.

It was no surprise that Matthew faced the challenge of overcoming testicular cancer in 2013 with the same determination and resolve that he has displayed throughout his rugby career, coming back to play again for Wales in 2014. His positive influence continues as a 37 year old playing today. I wish him and his family all the best.

Warren Gatland OBE
Head Coach of Wales
October 2018

CHAPTER 1

Parklands Playing Field to Sardis Road

MY ENTRY INTO this world was on 9th December 1980 in Church Village, in the County Borough of Rhondda Cynon Taf in Wales. I was born two months premature, weighing in at 5 lb 2 oz. I was the third sibling after Martin and Lisa – Julian would be the fourth child, but that would be a few years later. My mum, Alison, brought us up mainly on her own, with support from close relatives and grandparents. As you can imagine, a single mum bringing up four children is a challenge, especially with us kids constantly arguing and getting into fights like most siblings do. My dad, Paul, wasn't living with us, and we only saw him occasionally when I was young. I did get birthday cards, etc., but he wasn't a big part of my life. We lived on a council estate in Tonyrefail and had little money as my mum was a full-time parent, but we got by like a lot of families do when finances are tight.

I used to always be out with my best friends Ian and Daniel, be it playing football or rugby or just hanging around with them. Both are lifelong friends and their parents have been very good to me over the years. I was your standard sports-mad child, enjoying various different sports including athletics and tennis (during the Wimbledon fortnight), amongst others. I was also talented at field events such as the javelin, which

I participated in at my school, Tonyrefail Comprehensive. Football was also a sport I enjoyed, playing at centre-half for my school team. I carried on playing football until I was 15, but when I was required to decide between that and rugby, there was no contest. At the age of 11, whilst playing in the street with my friend Gareth – or Pudding, as he was nicknamed – he asked if I wanted to have a go at Rugby Union for Tonyrefail. I went along to training and the rest, as they say, is history. I'd found the sport that would change my life and become my profession, something unimaginable at the time.

One of the main reasons I went to play rugby was that I knew a few of my school friends, including my good mate Ian, would also be there so it was an opportunity to spend time with them. I had many school friends playing sports and a lot of nicknames were handed out. I was dubbed Smiler at the age of 11. I'm still unsure why the moniker was given to me. Yes, I did smile quite a bit, but so did all of my friends, so why I got that nickname is unclear to me. For many years, my wife has claimed it's because I never smile and that my friends were just being sarcastic, but I'm certain that's not the truth. What I do recognize is how absorbed in the sport we all were. Even when we weren't training for the rugby team, we'd be out on the street by our homes practising our passing and kicking skills.

We used to play with boys a bit older than ourselves in these games of 'grab rugby', as it was called, but by the end – boys being boys – it was full-on rugby, not played on grass but on the road outside our houses. On the odd occasion we also played rugby on a field with quite a steep incline, with those older than us in one team (with Pudding captaining the side) playing downhill while my team played uphill, and we hardly ever changed ends!

I'd invariably be one of Neil Jenkins, Scott Gibbs or Keith Wood, though if Jenks was still available by the time I got to pick who I was going to be, I'd normally choose him. Jenks at the time was playing for Pontypridd RFC and had just broken into the Welsh international set-up. I used to practise my passing and kicking for hours, and even when all my friends had gone home, or I was alone, I used to go to a local field to practise my kicking. Even now, if I was required to find touch with a clearing kick, or take on a straightforward penalty or conversion, I'd be confident I could do it. In later years I still used to practise my kicking with Jenks after training with Pontypridd and Celtic Warriors. The player I'd fantasised about being on the streets of Tonyrefail was now my colleague, something I could never have dreamed of all those years earlier.

In my initial season with Tonyrefail U11s, I must have played well as I received the 'most improved player of the season' award. Even in my first season of rugby union, my position was at hooker. I'm not like many others, who initially appeared in a different position and only found their strongest position in senior rugby. I played hooker from the start – the odd game at centre or flanker, but the vast majority at hooker – and I loved it. I loved the confrontational element of the role. I wasn't one of the biggest youngsters in the team, but I believed that I was a good player and I could stand up for myself even in those raw, inexperienced years. The team won more than they lost from U11s up to and including U16s level, with me as their kicker kicking many points in those years.

From U11s up to U15s level, our biggest adversaries were Dowlais and Pontyclun. I still vividly remember playing Dowlais at home when I was 14 or 15, and a fight breaking out in the top left-hand corner of the pitch – suddenly everyone was fighting on the adjacent children's play area where the swing, slides, etc. were – even some lads who weren't playing in the match! At U15s and U16s levels, Beddau had a very strong team. Playing for them were future stars such as Gethin Jenkins and Michael Owen, who'd progress to be internationals, plus Jason Simpson and Rhodri Morris – real stars in schoolboy rugby. The Tonyrefail U15s team were especially prominent in our area, and from about 14 or 15, my friends and I would go on Saturday afternoons to watch the senior side, Tonyrefail RFC, play if they were at home.

I was starting to get noticed for my rugby ability, and at 15 was chosen to represent Rhondda Schools and my County. In those teams, you could instantly feel that the level of performance was a notch up from what I'd encountered before. My schoolfriend Geraint Cook, also selected, and I realised we needed to train harder and get better. Cookie at that time was an outstanding rugby player, scoring countless tries and making clean breaks look effortless. Many at our school felt that Cookie would go on to represent his country at senior level. However, after youth rugby he just chose to stop playing – it just proves you never know who'll make it and who won't. Our new training sessions included weights to develop our strength, and we also used to strap tyres to ourselves with a belt and a rope to do sprinting drills. Another friend, Gareth Harding (who we just called Harding), and I used to run up a mountain with a sack on our backs, to see who'd be sick first. As part of our training regime, Harding and I also used to do weights in his dad's home gym – Harding always kept himself fit, helping push me along. He would have given anything to have played for Wales – he is a massive Ponty fan and very patriotic about his country. Harding's dad, who we called Kouff, was my Tonyrefail rugby coach from U11 up to U15 level.

I was determined to be the finest rugby player I could be – I've always believed in my ability. Growing up, the player I admired the most in my position as hooker was Keith Wood of Ireland. I loved the way he played in the set piece and in the loose. To improve our rugby skills, Geraint and I, and others, practised all aspects of the game. A lad who was a few years older than me and playing for Tonyrefail Youth spent many hours with me, practising our passing skills. I initially struggled to pass the ball off my left hand, but by the time I was 16, I could pass off both hands equally well. Even now in professional rugby, I still see players who struggle to pass off both hands.

Gethin Jenkins, a long-time friend of mine and, as mentioned earlier, an opponent when he played for Beddau at schoolboy level, also played for our County. When he was 15, Gethin was seemingly the second or third choice for the loosehead prop position, but eventually he did break into the team and they went all the way to the Dewar Shield Final. Gethin was left out of the team for the final, and to this day still talks about that final and the fact that he was dropped. A man who's won in excess of 100 caps for his country, and has been selected for the British and Irish Lions numerous times, still feels resentful over this. It just reveals the mark of the man – Melon, as he's known in rugby circles due to the size of his head, is one of the all-time greats of Welsh rugby. Another story from our youth involving Melon was when we were on tour with our County in Devon. Melon had a packet of biscuits and when Michael Owen and I tried to get them off him, he started crying – clearly you should never try to separate Melon from his biscuits.

At 16, I was invited to train with Welsh Schools: a very proud moment for me. I wasn't capped by Wales at that age group and was probably, in the selectors' eyes, fifth in line for the starting hooker position. As far as I was concerned, I was as good as if not better than the others in front of me, which suggested that perhaps their parents had the selectors' ears in trial games. None of my family members attended any of the training sessions, so who knows if things could have been different if they had.

A recollection that will always remain vividly with me is of a training camp at Sophia Gardens in Cardiff, where I had the task that nobody's ever wanted: holding the tackle pads for the first team to hit as hard as they can. The frustration was burning inside me, and at the end of a morning session on a Saturday, I made the decision to leave the camp and started walking home via Cathedral Road, where my mum picked me up. The following Monday at school I explained to a teacher what I'd done, and was told to write a letter of apology to Welsh Schools for my actions. Not the finest introduction to representative rugby for Wales, but fortunately that wasn't to be the end of representing my country.

Once we reached the age of 16, the team disbanded with players going to play for various sides in the area. I continued at Tonyrefail, playing for their Youth team. Every year whilst at Tonyrefail Youth, I had a trial for Pontypridd Youth. The first year I didn't get in, but did the second year, which I was thrilled about. One of my first games for Pontypridd Youth just happened to be against my friends at Tonyrefail Youth, which was a very strange experience.

I was equally delighted when I was selected in the squad for the Wales U18s age group in 1999. It seemed the tackle pads incident was long forgotten, or at least excused. I played two games for Wales U18s, against Australia and France. For my debut against Australia I was in the starting XV, with Michael Owen at number 8, and at scrum half, another future Wales player and British and Irish Lion, Dwayne Peel. Gethin Jenkins had to make do with a spot on the bench. In the Australian side was a flanker by the name of George Smith, who was to carve out quite a decent rugby career himself. Australia were much stronger and ran out 52-10 winners, myself and Dwayne each managing to grab a try in a very heavy loss. On a less happy note, there was an alley running next to our garden at the time, and after my mum washed my shirt from my Wales debut and hung it on the line to dry, it was stolen and never recovered.

Even though I'd now represented my country at an age group, I was still concerned that I wouldn't get to play at the top level in senior rugby. I was from a small village and felt that all the top players were either from a city or a town. What chance would a youngster born and living in the village of Tonyrefail have? But I was determined to give it my all – I had a burning ambition to play at the top level and for my country and if the opportunity came, I'd be ready. I do feel that nowadays lads who've represented their region or their country at age-group level often seem to consider they've made it: they're now established. This isn't the case: it's just the start of the journey, and there'll be many more challenges ahead before you've made it. In my view, only when you've played four years at the top level in your country's top league can you claim that you've established yourself.

I missed out on the Junior World Cup in 1999 – unfortunately, owing to the months it ran from and to, I was just too old for that tournament. This was a setback for me, in that I couldn't assess my talents against players of my age from other countries around the globe. I'd have to make do with playing for Pontypridd Youth against other Welsh guys, all hungry and eager to make the senior grade.

I kept up my steady progression through the age groups, and stepped up into Pontypridd U21s, who played on a Wednesday night, packing down once again with Melon. I also played twice for Tonyrefail RFC in the back row and hoped to stay there longer, but Clive Jones (overseeing Ponty at the time) told me I should be pushing myself to play at a higher level, and so I went on to play for Treorchy. The side was coached at the time by a man who'd had a good career in my position of hooker: Ian Greenslade, who'd played for Cardiff, Bridgend and Treorchy. Compo (as he's known) clearly saw potential in me. So I was playing Wednesday nights for Ponty U21s and for Treorchy on a Saturday. Both teams presented a considerable test for a young hooker like me, working to make my way in the game. The U21s were allowed to pick four overage players, so could select first team players who were out of form or players coming back from injuries, who savoured the chance to get stuck into inexperienced young players still learning their trade. With Treorchy, we were fortunate that in our ranks we had players such as Gavin Owen, Paul Dunning and Kevin Matthews – tough men who weren't going to let opposing players take liberties with their teammates.

My form was good and I was pleased with how I was playing and was enjoying my rugby. Around this time, I was made aware that Neath were interested in bringing in my services. Their coach at the time was ex-Wales international open-side flanker and Neath legend Lyn Jones. Neath were a considerable force in Welsh rugby and for them to show interest was a sizable boost to my confidence. I was very flattered and eager to see what they had to offer; that was until Pontypridd, a side I'd watched and admired, urged me to sign a senior contract. The youngster from Tonyrefail was being presented an opportunity to play senior top-flight Welsh rugby – one of my childhood dreams was on the brink of becoming reality.

Into the 2001–02 season, I was now part of the Pontypridd first team squad, as was Gethin, having both come up through the ranks at the club into the senior set-up. I had to pinch myself. I used to follow Pontypridd and their stars, such as Dale McIntosh (The Chief) and Neil Jenkins, on television in games such as the notorious 'Battle of Brive' and against Bath in the Heineken Cup when The Chief announced himself to the ribs of Bath blindside flanker Andy Robinson at Sardis Road. Memorable moments. And now I was practising with these same players and changing next to them in the changing room. I have to admit, at first I was overwhelmed. I wouldn't have said boo to a goose – I kept my head down and stayed quiet around the players who'd already established themselves in the game. I wasn't browbeaten or made to feel inferior amongst the players, it was just that you had to earn your right to be vocal in a changing room and around the place in those days. It's certainly different when an inexperienced player first enters a team nowadays, just showing the shifts in generations over the years.

The coach at Pontypridd when I broke into the first team squad was ex-Wales and Pontypridd (amongst other clubs) player Richie Collins. He didn't continue in that position for very long and was succeeded by Lynn Howells, a coach with a strong reputation. He'd previously been an assistant coach at Pontypridd, as well as coaching Wales' U21 and 'A' sides, then moving on to be assistant coach for Wales before coaching Cardiff, so had achieved a lot over the years. Clive Jones was also brought in as Director of Rugby, shaking things up at the club with his old-school standards. During his time coaching with his brother Chris at Treorchy, he had got them into the top flight of Welsh rugby. Both Clive and Chris had coached me with Rhondda Schools, so I knew them and their methods.

Pontypridd had a very useful side and we were successful that season. We won the Principality Cup at the Millennium Stadium (as they were then known), defeating Llanelli 20-17 in the final with a last-minute penalty by full back Brett Davey. That season Pontypridd also got to the final of the Parker Pen Shield, the second tier of European club competition, where we played Sale Sharks. Ponty defeated sides such as Saracens and London Irish to make the final at the Kassam Stadium in Oxford, where, in a very close game, we eventually succumbed to Sale 22-25. It was a truly disappointing result, as the winners automatically qualified for the Heineken European Cup, a tournament we were desperate to get back into. For a young hooker who was just starting out in his professional career, it was amazing to experience big games such as these – I look back and I'm still honoured to have made the match-day squad for these finals. I only played in a few games in my first season for Ponty, coming off the bench as a replacement in the Celtic League and as sub three times in the Parker Pen Shield. I was striving my hardest and was determined to play, but there was a fellow blocking my path who became a good mentor to me and played a considerable part in my advancement as a player.

Mefin Davies was the starting hooker for Ponty after his move from Neath. At the time Mefin was 29 and in great form, and was rewarded for this by breaking into the Welsh team for the first time. As a player, he wasn't the biggest in size but he was very durable – hardly ever injured. He was great with me, and always glad to answer any queries I had, whether it be advice about scrums or line-outs, or whatever. Mefin used to always say to me that 'set pieces are your priority – any other work you do around the park is a bonus', and it's a message I pass on to up-and-coming props and hookers to this day. Don't get me wrong: you still have to have all the other skill sets in terms of passing, ball carrying and tackling, etc. But as a hooker this is what you're judged on more than anything else – set pieces. Mefin was a superb tutor and an outstanding player. He carried on playing for Wales until he was 35, and was still playing top-flight rugby for the Ospreys at 39. I'd have to bide my time. I did make two starts in the Celtic League and one in the European Challenge Cup and was making progress in my overall game, but I was desperate to get more starts. Having said this, my determination and faith in my ability never waned.

I embraced my time at Pontypridd. We had a great bunch of boys, and I still think of travelling home from games with crates of lager and cider at the rear of the bus. One memory in particular sticks in my mind. After a team meeting for one of the games where Lynn had got us psyched up ready to play, we got on the bus and Team Manager Nigel Bezani – or Baz, as he's respectfully known in rugby circles – said 'Don't worry about tonight, I have two nightclubs for us to go to.' The other players and I were trying to get in the right frame of mind to do our best on the field, and Baz was planning our night out! Great moments and great memories, and I'm still in regular contact with players such as Dale McIntosh, Neil Jenkins and Phil Kingsley-Jones – all good friends of mine. But rugby union as we recognized it was about to evolve – it was 2003 and the game was about to be spun on its head. Regional rugby was coming to Wales.

CHAPTER 2

Celtic Warriors –
The Rise and Fall

IT WAS THE summer of 2003 and Welsh Rugby was going to change completely – regional rugby was upon us. Five regions were decided upon by the powers of Welsh rugby: Llanelli Scarlets, Cardiff Blues, Gwent Dragons, Neath-Swansea Ospreys and Celtic Warriors. When I heard this change was imminent, my first personal feeling was of panic. Would I even get a regional spot? If not, would I have to look over the Severn Bridge for a club to continue my progress as a rugby player – and might that hamper my dreams of playing for my country? Luckily, I'd received some reassurance from Lynn Howells. Lynn told me that Steve Hansen, the Wales coach, had been impressed by my style of play in a few training sessions the previous season that I'd participated in with the Wales squad, and my performances with Pontypridd had also had a positive effect. I was told that the WRU had, before the previous season had ended, put together lists of players and organised them into three separate categories from the viewpoint of looking towards regional rugby. Category A was for international players, Category B was for players who they believed had the potential to become international players, and then finally Category C was for players who they deemed would probably remain club/regional players. I was informed that I'd been placed in Category B, and Lynn was very confident I had nothing to be concerned about. The day when the players were advised individually – face to face with Lynn and Gareth Thomas, the Chief Executive of Pontypridd – on whether they were going to be offered a regional contract was still a nervous time, though. I was so happy when I heard that I was going to be part of the Celtic Warriors regional squad – though at that point the name still hadn't been decided upon for the upcoming season, the first of regional rugby.

The two main aims behind the change to regional rugby were to improve domestic rugby performance levels in order to be more competitive with other sides in Europe that were progressing quickly, plus – with limited resources financially – only having five regions rather than the previous nine top-level clubs would mean that the money could be distributed over a smaller number. The idea was that these two changes would combine to improve the performance of the national side. In the summer of 2003, clubs which had historically been at the top table of Welsh rugby were now being downgraded to semi-professional sides, a massive transformation for the game and for the Welsh public. Historic powerhouses of Welsh rugby such as Pontypridd, Pontypool, Maesteg and Aberavon (just to name a few) were now being downgraded to the second tier of the Welsh domestic game – how would fans of the Welsh game react? We were about to find out.

I was 23 years of age and, as I said, was delighted to be included in the Celtic Warriors playing squad. In my position, I was in competition with Mefin Davies (again), Andrew Joy, Duane Goodfield and Chris Balshen. I was looking forward to the upcoming season and being coached yet again by my coach at Pontypridd, Lynn Howells, as well as by Allan Lewis, an outstanding coach. With Lynn and Allan it was very much a good cop, bad cop combination: they were a great partnership. Bringing together a region made up of Bridgend and Pontypridd players was always going to be a challenge, but with Lynn in charge and the fact that the previous year Bridgend had won the Welsh League, as a group of players we felt that we were in a good place. Celtic Warriors were officially the region covering Mid-Glamorgan – so I was playing for my local region, being a Tonyrefail boy – and also the South Powys area. Our training base was at Pencoed College, and there was a good feel around the players and the coaches.

Three regions – Neath-Swansea Ospreys, Gwent Dragons and Celtic Warriors – were combining clubs, while Cardiff Blues and the Llanelli Scarlets stood alone, each as an individual entity. Fans of the amalgamated regions were struggling with the new approach. The name of the new region was a contentious issue, as were the team colours we were going to wear – you had Bridgend with their traditional blue and white kit, and Pontypridd with their white and black kits. Also, where were our home games going to be played, at the Brewery Field or at Sardis Road? Fans wanted to know the answers to all these questions. Eventually, Celtic Warriors was agreed on as the name, the home kit would be blue, black and white and the games would be divided between the two stadiums. Fans in the main were happy with these options in comparison with other options being bandied around, and as a group of players we were looking forward to the first season of regional rugby.

The pre-season started off really badly for me, though. I had a painful groin injury, diagnosed as osteitis pubis, which meant the whole pre-season was a write-off, as I was unable to run. To make matters worse, I was made aware that I was on the verge of a Wales call-up for the summer tour to Australia. I was asked to attend a meeting with Wales physio Mark Davies to assess my fitness. Carcass (as Mark's known) ruled me out of the tour, which was obviously a huge disappointment at the time. I eventually returned to action two or three games into the season, so I had a bit of catching up to do in terms of general fitness, but I couldn't wait to get the boots on and get out on the rugby field with the boys.

Our first game in the Celtic League was at Netherdale in the Scottish Borders, home of Gala RFC. They're a historic

Scottish team where international players of the calibre of Gregor Townsend, Peter Brown and David Leslie all played, to name a few. With myself injured and Mefin unavailable due to World Cup duty, Duane Goodfield started at hooker for the Warriors, and we came away with a convincing victory against Scottish regional side The Borders, winning 49-12. There were tries from Tongan international Aisea Havili, Gareth Wyatt and Nick Kelly, and a brace from Shaun James. Neil Jenkins was accurate from the tee as always, with three conversions and six penalties. With Jenks in your team, you always had a chance and he was fantastic for us, as he was throughout his career. In the week building up to the first game there was a lot of press coverage, with Bridgend owner Leighton Samuel stating that with the way finances were at Pontypridd, Bridgend would become the dominant partner in the region. Little did we know then that finances would continue to pose issues throughout the season and eventually be the destroyer for the region.

Our first home game was the following week against Leinster at Sardis Road. In a tight game, Gareth Wyatt scored a try right at the conclusion of the game to take the win 29-22. We beat Leinster home and away that season, as well as completing the double over Cardiff Blues, amongst many other victories. In the game at Cardiff Arms Park, Alfie scored a hat-trick of tries. I made my first start for the region in October, away to Ulster at Ravenhill. My opposing number was Paul Shields, who was an Irish international. We lost 26-20 but I was satisfied with how I performed that day and was looking forward to more opportunities. Unfortunately, only a month before I made my full debut for the Celtic Warriors, Pontypridd was wound up as a partner in the region, due to outstanding debts. Leighton Samuel wished to pay off the debt and take sole ownership of the Celtic Warriors, but, the WRU blocked this action as they wanted the region run on a 50:50 ownership basis. What then occurred is that Samuel bought the Pontypridd debt and gave it as a gift to the WRU, meaning that now the Celtic Warriors were co-controlled by Samuel and the WRU, but with Samuel stipulating that all home games would now be played at the Brewery Field in Bridgend. The Pontypridd fans were very unhappy at this decision and made their sentiments known at the final league game played at Sardis Road, where we defeated the Newport Gwent Dragons (as they became known in August 2003). The players thought at the time that these off-field issues were just initial teething issues with a new region – we had no idea of the seriousness of the matter at this point, or in fact right until the very end.

In the Celtic League, we finished in a very creditable fourth place, winning 14 out of the 22 league games played, Llanelli Scarlets taking the league title. Neil Jenkins finished as the league's top points scorer in his final season. We were pleased with how we'd performed in our first season: we really stepped up and were competitive in all the matches we played.

I can honestly say, looking back over my career, that the group of players at the Celtic Warriors are up there with the very best I've played with. We had international stars such as Gareth 'Alfie' Thomas, Gareth Cooper, Neil Jenkins, Sonny Parker, Kevin Morgan, Dafydd James, Maama Molitika and Gethin Jenkins. The spirit and strength in depth were excellent. If we had injuries to our starting centres Dafydd James and Sonny Parker, then we had as replacements players such as Jonny Bryant and David Bishop, who'd do a great job. At scrum half, if Gareth Cooper wasn't available, we had Sililo Martens or Paul John to step in to play; all three were international players in their own right. We were a very good side, full of internationals and well captained by Richard Bryan or Alfie, and we felt we could achieve some real success with this group.

That season in Europe in the Heineken Cup, we were drawn in the same pool as London Wasps, French club Perpignan and Italian club Calvisano. It was a tough group, with only the pool winners assured a place in the quarter-finals. We defeated Calvisano home and away and beat Perpignan by a point at home before losing away to the French side, who had a juggernaut pack performing that day and in the backs, controlling things, the mercurial talent of Australian fly half Manny Edmonds. Our pack that day was me in between Christian Loader and Gethin Jenkins, who had an outing at tight-head prop. Second rows were Brent Cockbain and Robert Sidoli, with a back row of Maama Molitika, Richard Parks and Cory Harris. It was a really physical game, and I'll never forget their lock, Christophe Porcu, going around throwing punches at quite a few of the lads – he was definitely on a mission that day. Melon took a smack off him in that game, and was knocked out! Actually, that day Melon was sparked out twice, by two different Perpignan players: welcome to playing in France! We gave as good as we got, but we were on the wrong side of the scoreline. After the game, Celtic Warriors cited Porcu and following a hearing he was rightfully banned for five weeks for continuous foul play.

The other highly regarded side in our pool was London Wasps, who had a star-studded side with players such as World Cup winners Josh Lewsey and Lawrence Dallaglio, as well as other stars such as Craig Dowd, Trevor Leota, Simon Shaw, Joe Worsley, Kenny Logan and Rob Howley. They'd ultimately go on to win the final with the famous Howley try when Clément Poitrenaud was caught napping behind his try line. Our first encounter with them was away, and in a tight affair, a try by Aisea Havili made the difference. We came away with a 14-9 victory: a really great success against an established top side.

The following week, we played them again at the Brewery Field to a packed-out crowd. The fans were delighted, not just from the win the previous week, but because of the breaking news that the rumoured merging of the Celtic Warriors with the Cardiff Blues wasn't going to take place. As players we were as much in the dark as our fans. We didn't know if there was any substance to the rumours or not – as far as we knew, all was well with the region. The boys were really fired-up for this game, and there were a few altercations going on all the way through. Nick Kelly, a replacement for injured Brent Cockbain at lock, was engaged in a fight with Lawrence Dallaglio, with

Nick pinning Dallaglio to the ground and landing a few shots. Richard Parks tried in vain to get Nick off Dallaglio – Parksey seemed to find this more of a challenge than the endurance events he's since taken part in all over the world: he just couldn't dislodge him. Gethin also got into a quarrel with the English international, as did Chris Horsman, who after being on the field for only seven minutes after replacing Christian Loader, was sin-binned for a challenge on Dallaglio. This certainly caught the England number 8's attention, as he was also sin-binned not too much later on for a late tackle on our winger Gareth Wyatt. Through all this, nevertheless, Wasps played a better game on the day and took the victory 17-12. Unfortunately, the two losses to Perpignan and London Wasps cost us a pass to the later stages. We finished second in the group, Wasps winning it and going on to be European Champions, with Welshman Rob Howley starring and future Wales coaches in Warren Gatland and Shaun Edwards at the helm. London Wasps only lost one game in the whole tournament – to us. We'd shown everyone over the two matches and with our performances in the Celtic League how competitive we were already against the very best rugby sides in Europe. Things looked really encouraging.

As detailed throughout this chapter, the players heard many rumours of issues with funds and the prospect of the region being no more, but we were constantly being assured that there was nothing to worry about regarding the future of the Celtic Warriors. We obviously knew that Ponty's shares in the Celtic Warriors had been sold to the WRU and that they were in partnership with Leighton Samuel. We were being regularly told that all was well and that we'd have the opportunity to develop on our first season as a team. I, and others, felt we were on the verge of an exciting period for the Celtic Warriors.

However, the rumours of issues off the field wouldn't go away. On a few occasions pay cheques initially bounced when you went to pay them into your bank account, but then the problem was resolved. As a group of players and coaches, we started to push Samuel more for answers, and had a number of meetings with him at the Decor Frame factory he owned in Bridgend. Samuel spoke to the group and reiterated that he was going to run the region in partnership with the WRU and there was nothing to worry about.

For the final game of the season we played Connacht in Galway, and won convincingly. After the game we stayed overnight as Mefin was getting married that summer, so we had his stag do there in Ireland, which was a great night. When we got back, we were looking forward to having the summer off, spending time with the family, going on holiday and chilling out before returning to Celtic Warriors for another season, and looking to improve on our first. Ryan Jones and I had been offered a three-year contract extension on improved terms with the Warriors, and we were both happy with the details and looking to sign the contract in the coming weeks. Oh, if we'd only known what bombshell was around the corner...

A few days after getting back from Ireland, I got a phone call from Ryan Jones to tell me that all players had been asked to attend a compulsory meeting at the Vale Hotel. When I got there, all the players were milling around, and when all were there, we were told that the Celtic Warriors would be no more. Our players' representative was Richard Harry, and he informed us that in a separate area of the hotel all the Chief Executives from the other four regions were going through the players and deciding which ones to recruit for their respective regions. It was that ruthless. We were advised that if another region wanted our services, we'd be offered the same length of contract and terms as our current contract with the Celtic Warriors – meaning that if Ryan and myself were offered another Welsh region, it would be on the terms of our existing contract, not the new contract we hadn't yet signed. Players were stunned. Livelihoods were on the line, with mortgages to be paid, and we as professionals were waiting in that hotel for a decision to be made on each of us individually.

The players were invited one by one into a room where Richard Harry and Steve Lewis, Chief Executive of the

WRU, would advise if one or more regions wanted you, and it was then down to the player and his agent to talk to those interested. As for the contracts being on the same terms, this actually turned out not to be the case. The regions realised that most rival clubs outside of Wales had already decided on their playing staff for the next season, putting them in a very strong negotiating position. Players were offered contracts on less advantageous terms than their existing Celtic Warriors contracts in many cases, and it was a matter of take it, or leave it and run the risk of not finding another club outside of Wales. I was fortunate: Llanelli Scarlets wanted me to move to them, and I was advised to travel to Llanelli to discuss the move with coaches Gareth Jenkins and Nigel Davies.

Only three players from Celtic Warriors were going to the Scarlets. Arwel Thomas had just signed with us, replacing the retiring Neil Jenkins. He had been keen to return to Wales after his stint in France with Pau, and now he'd got himself caught up in this situation. Luckily Scarlets wanted him too, as well as Aisea Havili, the Tongan international. Some players weren't so fortunate. Mefin was the first-choice hooker for Wales at that time, but wasn't offered a contract by any of the regions and ended up playing for Neath, before being picked up by Gloucester a year later. We were all devastated – none of the players or coaches could believe it had come to this. Tellingly, Leighton Samuel was nowhere to be seen that day.

Looking back now, it's crazy how things ended up like this. We'd been lied to by Samuel numerous times. He was a businessman who shouldn't have been put in such an important role within Welsh rugby, in charge of 40 to 50 professional sportsmen. The players and coaches were badly let down, and we've never received our salary for that final month of being employed by the Celtic Warriors. A poor end to what had promised so much on the rugby field with such a great bunch of boys. Despite the sour ending, I can honestly say I loved my time with the Celtic Warriors – one of the most talented squads of players I've had the good fortune to play with.

CHAPTER 3

Becoming a Scarlet –
The Gareth Jenkins Years

JOINING LLANELLI SCARLETS was a massive move for me and I went there initially with a few concerns playing on my mind. I believed in my rugby ability, but after the turmoil of the Celtic Warriors, I was going to a club where I hardly knew anyone, which I found unsettling. I did know Dwayne Peel from playing at youth level with Wales and I'd met Gareth Jenkins, who was now going to become my Director of Rugby at the Scarlets. Whilst playing for Rhondda U16s quite a few years earlier, I'd been introduced to Gareth after the game and, by all accounts, he was impressed with me as a player. This did provide me with some reassurance, but his initial analysis was going to be put to the test on a much bigger stage.

Arwel Thomas had the difficult task of replacing Stephen Jones at the club, Stephen having made the decision to move to France to ply his trade for Clermont Auvergne. So poor Arwel, who'd come from France initially to replace the fly-half legend that was Neil Jenkins at the Celtic Warriors only for that to go sour, was now replacing another legend at fly half for the Scarlets! Some people have all the luck!

The previous season, the Scarlets had won the Celtic League and also reached the quarter-finals of the Heineken Cup, losing to French side Biarritz. They had high hopes of a successful season and I was looking forward to playing a big part in that success. In the squad there were some outstanding players, such as Simon Easterby, Dafydd Jones, Chris Wyatt, Vernon Cooper, John Davies, Iestyn Thomas, Dwayne Peel, a young up-and-coming scrum half called Mike Phillips, Mark Jones, Mark Taylor, Andy Powell, Scott Quinnell, Salesi Finau, Regan King, Barry Davies and Lee Byrne, just to name a few. The region was ambitious and had a really talented group of players and I felt I was joining at just the right time.

When I spoke to the two coaches, Gareth Jenkins and Nigel Davies, it was made clear to me that I was coming in as third-choice hooker. The club already had Welsh international Robin McBryde, and his back-up, Aled Gravelle, was seen as the future of the region, with the plan being that he'd take over the number 2 shirt when Robin was either away on international duty or unavailable. This situation didn't put me off the move: I accepted that I only had one year of regional rugby under my belt at this point, but I also knew if I got the opportunity, I was going to make the most of it. At the Celtic Warriors, with Mef away on World Cup duty, I'd been given the chance by Lynn Howells to play games which had given me a lot of experience and confidence, and I felt I was ready to take on Robin and Aled. Initially the plan was for me to play for Llandovery RFC, who were affiliated with the Scarlets, to gain game time as a third-choice hooker for a region often does, but as it panned out I didn't turn out for Llandovery once during my time with the Scarlets. I did play once for the Carmarthen Quins for 30 minutes against Aberavon Quins, but bar that one time, I remained with the region throughout my time there. It just shows that things don't always work out as planned.

That first pre-season with the Scarlets was a real eye-opener to me. I'd hardly participated in the pre-season before due to my groin injury, so this was my first proper pre-season of regional rugby. The fitness coach for the Scarlets was Wayne Proctor, himself a Welsh international and Llanelli star who'd only recently retired from rugby. Prior to pre-season training,

I'd been on a two-week all-inclusive holiday to Mexico and on my first day of training with the Scarlets, I was asked to do 30 x100 m runs. I was really struggling with the last few and Robin McBryde helped me complete the task – welcome to training with the Scarlets! The sessions were difficult but the running, and other aspects of the training we were doing, was turning us into a side with great levels of fitness. The tradition with Llanelli rugby, constantly encouraged by Gareth Jenkins, was that if you saw an opportunity to move the ball wide, you should take the opportunity. The message was very much giving responsibility to the player, and telling us not to be afraid to try to take an opponent on. And with our backs, in particular, we had people who were more than capable of beating an adversary and scoring some great tries. The one player who I really admired right from those first days at the Scarlets was Regan King. Capped just once for New Zealand (ironically, against Wales), he was just a fantastic rugby player – one of the most, if not the most, gifted I've ever played with. I'd have paid money just to watch him train to see some of the things he did. Truly a great player and one of the best ever to don that famous Scarlets shirt.

Unfortunately for him but fortunately for me, Robin was struggling with a neck injury and I was showing up well in training. I felt really good and a full pre-season was really helping me. I travelled back and forth from the Valleys to Llanelli in a car with other Scarlets players. Over the years this car-sharing group included the likes of Chris Wyatt, Iestyn Thomas, Barry Davies, Mike Phillips, Jonathan Edwards, Gareth Maule and Rhys Thomas. Mauley was a hell of a character who was always trying to outdo you. Johnny Edwards was tight and if he was doing the driving then he wouldn't rush, to be economical with fuel. Rhys Thomas was always late for lifts, and after a few warnings was told if late again, he'd have to make his own way, which he did end up having to do a few times. Chris was a smoker and was allowed two cigarettes in the car whilst we travelled to training – not the healthiest start to your day! On some occasions on journey back would stop off at Jenkins Bakery in Llanelli for a pick-me-up after training. During the car journeys we talked about all sorts, and there was a great camaraderie between those of us who travelled together over the years in that car.

I was selected to make my debut for the Scarlets against Narberth, and I felt overall it went quite well. A few weeks later I was selected to start at Stradey Park against London Wasps. A match had been put together between the previous season's English League Champions and Celtic League Champions – the inaugural Anglo-Celtic Challenge. I was looking forward to facing London Wasps, who weren't just the reigning English Champions but the European Champions as well. London Wasps fielded players such as Josh Lewsey, Tom Voyce, Matt Dawson, Joe Worsley and Lawrence Dallaglio that day, and in direct opposition to me was the Samoan international Trevor Leota. He had a reputation at the time of being quite a handful and a huge tackler (not always legal). We had a decent side out ourselves, with Taylor and Finau in the centre, Mike Phillips at scrum half and Gareth Bowen captaining the side at fly half. Right throughout the season Gareth and Ceiron Thomas would push Arwel all the way as the man to replace Stephen Jones in the number 10 shirt, and it was an interesting battle. We had a good pack with Iestyn Thomas and Canadian Jon Thiel either side of me: both very strong, solid props. Vernon Cooper and Adam Jones formed the second row and we had a ball-carrying back row in the shape of Andy Powell, Scott Quinnell and Gavin Thomas. The game was really close and going into the last ten minutes we were leading by two points, but then Mike Phillips got sin-binned (unlike him to get involved in anything like that). We eventually lost to a late Tom Voyce try by a scoreline of 17 points to 20. Pushing the European Champions that close gave us real confidence, and we had a lot of belief in ourselves going into the season.

However, the 2004–05 season was one mainly of disappointment for the Scarlets. I'm not looking for excuses, but we had a number of injuries and just didn't seem to get any consistency in our performances. In the Celtic League, we finished in a disappointing fifth position, so not a great defence of our title from the previous year. In the Heineken Cup, we didn't get out of the pool stages; finishing third in our pool, which also included Toulouse, Northampton Saints and Glasgow. Our first game was at Stradey Park against Toulouse, a game that was tight all the way through, but the boot of French international scrum half Jean-Baptiste Élissalde got them over the line by 9 points to 6. We followed this up with a heavy defeat in round two, away at Franklin Gardens to Northampton Saints, by 25 points to 3. The Saints were physically stronger and better than us, which was a wake-up call re where we had to get to.

When you lose your first two games in Europe, you really are stuck in a bad place and it's hard to come back from that kind of start. We did beat Glasgow both home and away in the next round, but were then narrowly defeated at home by Northampton Saints, which ended any hopes we had of getting out of the pool. The following week we travelled to Toulouse, who by this point were one of the favourites to win the whole competition, and the game turned out to be a classic.

Stade Ernest Wallon's a great stadium to play at, and that day in January 2005 was no exception. I was happily selected to start, with both Robin and Aled Gravelle on the bench. As mentioned earlier, we had a number of injuries during the season and that game was no different, with several players not available for selection. To give you an example of this, lining up at centre that day was Mike Phillips, a player who played in that position a few times later in his career – once famously for the British and Irish Lions – but as a less experienced player, being asked to play there against a star-studded side like Toulouse is a big ask. Luckily, Mike being Mike, he's not fazed by much and dealt very well with their twin centre threat of French internationals Yannick Jauzion and Florian Fritz – two exceptional players, especially Jauzion, who at that time was a world-class operator. The Toulouse side then was magnificent, with a roster of players in addition to the two centres including Gareth Thomas, Vincent Clerc, Élissalde, William Servat, Fabien Pelous, Trevor Brennan and the Maka brothers, Finau and Isitolo, just to name a few. That day, New Zealand tight-head prop Carl Hayman, rightfully recognised as one of the all-time greats in that position, had to make do with a place on the bench. It just shows how strong they were at that time – a huge challenge for any team in Europe to face.

We got off to a great start and scored a try in the early minutes when Clément Poitrenaud, prone to silly errors mixed in with absolute brilliance, threw out a hopeful lofted pass. This was intercepted by Chris Wyatt, who galloped in for a try. Chris scored two tries in that game – he was a great athlete and really enjoyed himself that day. Being a regular smoker certainly didn't seem to affect his performances! The game was a try-fest, with Toulouse scoring eight tries, including one from Alfie, and us five – thirteen in total: some game! We showed great character that day and just kept going – scoring five tries at Toulouse is no mean feat. However, a loss is a loss and losing 53 points to 36 hurt a whole lot. Toulouse went on to win the final against Stade Français to become European Champions. We'd get revenge at Stade Ernest Wallon, but we had go through some losses against them both home and away first.

As we finished fifth in the Celtic League, we qualified for the Celtic Cup: a competition for the teams who finished in the top six. The cup competition was played at the end of the season. After defeating Newport Gwent Dragons and then beating the Ospreys, we were in the final at Lansdowne Road, where we'd face Munster. The game was Alan Gaffney's last in charge of Munster before he returned to Australia, and they had all their stars on show, which meant players such as Rob Henderson, Ronan O'Gara, Peter Stringer, Marcus Horan, Donncha O'Callaghan, Alan Quinlan, David Wallace and the late great, Anthony 'Axel' Foley. The side was led by Paul O'Connell, a true great of the Irish game. I got the start over

Aled, with Robin being unavailable. We had a good side out, with Mike back at 9, and Ceiron Thomas getting the start at 10. We had a dangerous back three if we could secure good ball for them: Barry Davies, Garan Evans and Aisea Havili. We were captained by Irishman Simon Easterby, who was a fantastic player and a great leader of the team, and we felt even though we were playing Munster in Ireland, we had a great chance. We pushed Munster all the way but in the end lost the final by 27 points to 16. It was a disappointing end to the season for the club, but at least I'd played in many more games than I'd expected before the season started. I'd also been involved in Wales squads and was going to be off that summer with them to North America, full of hope that I'd get to play for my country (this is covered in Chapter 5).

The 2005–06 season wasn't long underway when we received news that had been feared for a while. Robin McBryde was going to have to retire from rugby due to an injury at the top of his spine, which he'd undergone an unsuccessful operation to try to resolve. Robin was a great player. A Welsh international and a British and Irish Lions tourist, it was a real shame he had to retire. He'd been a great servant to Welsh rugby as a player and retiring gave him the opportunity to become a coach, which has taken him into coaching at international level for his beloved country.

The season was again disappointing for the region. We finished sixth in the Celtic League, so one place worse than the year before. In the Heineken Cup, we again failed to get out of our pool, which consisted of Toulouse (again), London Wasps and Edinburgh. We started our campaign in Toulouse, where Aled Gravelle got the start at hooker. Toulouse were again superb, scoring seven tries and winning by 50 points to 26, with Alfie again getting on the scoresheet with a try after a fantastic team move. I came on for John Davies and had a stint at prop whilst he got stitched up – luckily for me it was uncontested scrums, due to there not being enough recognised props on the pitch. Losing for the second consecutive year by such a large margin was very hard to take. The following week we defeated Edinburgh at Stradey Park in a narrow victory and next up were our old friends London Wasps in a game we needed to win.

The game against London Wasps at Stradey Park was a daytime match with the stadium packed. The game started in good weather, but by half-time the stadium and surrounding areas were cloaked in a dense fog and you couldn't see five yards in front of you. We went into the game knowing we had to win to keep our hopes alive, and knew we were in for a tough afternoon against a team with their capabilities. We managed to get the win in tough conditions and I had a great battle with French star, Raphaël Ibañez. John Davies had a fantastic game, rolling back the years, scrummaging well and getting his hands on the ball with some great carries. Mark Jones, not long back after a long absence with a knee injury, scored a stunning try, racing past Mark van Gisbergen and evading Paul Sackey's desperate attempt to tackle him. The match ended with a 21 points to 13 victory to us. The following weekend we'd have to do it again at the Causeway Stadium against the same opponents, as is always the case with games in early to mid-December in the Heineken Cup. The question was, could we back up our home win against them?

I again got the start, but London Wasps that day were a totally different proposition from what they'd been in the game only one week earlier. On this occasion they took us apart. They scored six tries, including a hat trick from Tom Voyce and a stunning solo effort by Josh Lewsey. We were blown away. Our team had some great players, but we just couldn't maintain a top level of performance against the very best sides. We were coming up short and were determined to change this.

In early January 2006 it was announced that Stephen Jones would be returning to the Scarlets at the start of the next season. This was great news for us. Stephen was a fantastic player, and though Gareth Bowen, Arwel Thomas, Ceiron Thomas and Mike Hercus all had their moments in the number 10 shirt, we now had a true international-calibre player to partner Dwayne Peel at half back. This would give us real control in those positions, which are key for any side. Dwayne had fought off Mike Phillips for the starting number 9 shirt and Mike had left to join the Cardiff Blues, to try and get regular games so he could push to become the starting Wales scrum half.

That month we lost by a point to Edinburgh in the Heineken Cup, which was a major disappointment. The following week we had Toulouse coming to Llanelli, and I was as determined as my teammates to put in a massive performance – no matter what our position in the pool – against a team who'd given us some real hidings.

Held on a bright winter day in Llanelli, the game was another fantastic showdown between us and them, with both teams playing some great attacking rugby. We scored only 47 seconds in, after a great pass from Dwayne which set Barry Davies on his way to the line. Barry scored two tries that day, and showed his great running ability in attack throughout the contest. Martyn Madden, our barnstorming prop, scored a try after great work from the centre magician Regan King, and we were constantly causing their defence problems. Toulouse also scored some great tries including four from Vincent Clerc. The final scoreline was Llanelli Scarlets 42 Toulouse 49, in what was a great game to be part of. Admittedly, it was another defeat against them, but we'd really pushed them and at least they hadn't scored 50 points this time!

Again, as per the season before, our performances in Europe and the Celtic League were disappointing. We did have some success in another cup competition, the Anglo-Welsh Cup. In the semi-final in late March, we defeated Bath by 27 points to 26 at the Millennium Stadium in front of over 50,000 fans, and suddenly we were all looking forward to a trip to Twickenham to take on London Wasps once more. In the end, the final was dominated by London Wasps and they ran out 26 points to 10 winners. This capped off a season where we came up short; very frustrating for the players and I'm sure the fans.

On the Welsh international front, there were changes afoot in the coaching area. With Mike Ruddock – after a Grand Slam-winning Six Nations – leaving his post, the rumours were rife that our Director of Rugby, Gareth Jenkins, was in line for the role. Gareth had applied previously and had been considered the favourite, only for Mike to be offered the job. In late April 2006, it was confirmed by the Welsh Rugby Union that Gareth was going to be taking over with Wales and that the Scarlets would therefore need a new man at the helm. Gareth was a great coach and Director of Rugby, for Llanelli originally and then with the regional side, Llanelli Scarlets. He was very passionate about the game and a great motivator; a great man-manager. He understood players and gave them breaks from rugby when they needed it to get their bodies right; or if he felt training was going well and people were ready, giving them a day away from training to rest. He was great for me at Scarlets. I'll talk about his Wales coaching career in Chapters 5 and 6, but a new man was now required to come in and build on what Gareth had already done with the Scarlets.

CHAPTER 4

A New Man in Charge –
A Change of Fortune in Europe

GOING INTO THE pre-season of the 2006–07 season, we still didn't have a coach at the helm. Following Gareth Jenkins' appointment as Wales Coach, Nigel Davies had also gone over to the national side as Assistant Coach so a totally new management level was required. In August, it was announced that ex-Llanelli forward and Welsh international Phil Davies would become the new Director of Rugby, replacing Gareth. Phil had done a remarkable job with Leeds, transforming them from a fourth division club to a team playing in the top division of the English League, and was highly thought of. Supporting coaches were also put in place, with Paul Moriarty remaining and Robert Jones moving to skills coach. Both were very well-respected. Anthony Buchanan, an ex-Llanelli and Welsh international prop, came in to support us with scrum advice one day a week. All in all, it was a good group of knowledgeable rugby men with a wealth of experience.

The boys warmed to the new coaches well and once again, there were high hopes going into the new season. We felt we had a good squad of players with some now at the peak of their careers, and with Stephen Jones now back, we felt we had that little bit extra in terms of ability to make us a real force. Replacing an integral part of the club like Gareth, who'd been in charge as either coach or Director of Rugby for Llanelli and Llanelli Scarlets for 24 years, having also been a player there for 9 years, was never going to be easy. Being a former player and captain for Llanelli, Phil knew the surroundings and had the respect of the players and fans, which certainly helped, but results were what he'd be rated against and he knew that better than anyone. As part of the pre-season, we were facing a game against Gloucester away. The day before the game, the team had a training session at Swansea University and Phil asked us all to run 3K around the university playing fields. Although we were wondering why we were doing this a day before the game, we started running with no complaining. It turned out that Phil was just testing our mind-set, to see if we'd follow his instruction. He told us all to stop after two laps, happy that his men had followed his request.

We kicked off our league campaign against Ulster at Ravenhill. We had a few players missing through injury but others coming in from the academy, including full back Martyn Thomas, lock Lou Reed, winger Darren Daniel and centre Gavin Evans. I started at hooker and sitting on the bench waiting for his opportunity we had a young up-and-coming hooker, Ken Owens, who turned out to be not a bad player at all. Ulster had a fine team at the time and deserved the victory by 31 points to 16. After just one game, we were under no illusion about the hard work that lay ahead.

Next we played our first home league game of the season against Glasgow Warriors. Before the game, fans were handed leaflets detailing the club's plans to move to a new ground and sell the historic Stradey Park to housing developers. The reason given was that as resources stood, there was a real risk of the region going under unless this happened. My initial thoughts were, "Here we go again!", but I was determined to concentrate on playing and try to take the attitude of 'what will be, will be' off the field. There was a lot of resistance from the fans to the idea of the club moving from Stradey Park, not just due to not wanting to leave their historic home but also because it was felt that the roads and infrastructure wouldn't cope with building over 400 new homes in the area. The businessmen running the region would have a battle on their hands winning the fans over. At least we beat Glasgow 31 points to 17, earning our first league points of the season, which was a good win and got us up and running.

The League campaign went quite well that year. We finished in fourth place, winning 12 of our 20 league games, an improvement on the previous two seasons. However, it was in Europe where we really showed how good a team we could be, and that season will be remembered for many years to come.

The Heineken Cup draw put us in the same pool as our frequent opponents in Europe, Toulouse, plus Ulster and London Irish. They were all good sides but we felt we had a real chance of qualifying from the pool. First up was London Irish at the Madejski Stadium. We got off to a great start, playing some really good rugby, and after 75 minutes we were cruising 32-6 up after tries by Simon Easterby and Mark Jones – who scored a great individual try – and a rare one from Iestyn Thomas. Stephen Jones was deadly with his goal kicking and things were looking very good. Although we conceded 19 points in the last five minutes, we managed to hold on to the win and I picked up the Man of the Match award. Leaving Reading that evening we were happy to get the win but disappointed with how we'd let them back into the game in the final five minutes, almost costing us a victory, so there were mixed feelings within the group. However, it was a great start for us to beat a very good London Irish team.

Next up was Ulster at Stradey Park and we put in a good performance, winning 21 points to 15 with tries from Regan King and Mark Jones. Stephen Jones was again excellent with his goal kicking and his all-round performance, as he so often was. Two wins from two in Europe – very different from the previous two campaigns, and there was a great feeling around the place. Before the next round of matches in Europe took place, it was announced that the region had secured the investment to build a new stadium and had big, ambitious plans off the pitch as well as on it. As players, we just had to concentrate on our performances and in Europe next up at home were going to be the team that had caused us so much pain in recent years: French side Toulouse.

The game started really well for us – we scored a try through lock forward Scott MacLeod after a wayward line-out from Toulouse. With Stephen Jones converting the try and scoring a couple of penalties, we were 13 points up and feeling pretty good about ourselves. Being the class side they are, though, Toulouse came back with tries from Vincent Clerc and Clément Poitrenaud. Clerc then scored another try and suddenly the game was flipped on its head. We managed to come back and score a try late on through Simon Easterby after great work firstly by Dafydd James and then supported by the whole back row, with Alix Popham and Gavin Thomas freeing the third man of their trio, Easterby, to score.

Right at the end their fly half, South African Gaffie du Toit, pinged us back on our line with a great touch-finding kick. Being only one point up, we wondered if yet again we were going to fall to them. Du Toit had an attempted drop goal blocked and a long-range effort very late on from Clerc didn't worry the posts, and finally we'd gained a victory over them, with a final scoreline of Scarlets 20 Toulouse 19. Obviously we were all delighted, but only three games into the campaign there was still a long way to go – plus we had only seven days before we had to go to Toulouse to take them on again in their own backyard.

Stade Ernest-Wallon, Toulouse, 16th December 2006: a day that will long be remembered by Scarlets fans and indeed rugby fans in general, no matter who you support. We went into the game undefeated in Europe after 3 games, but we knew from previous encounters what a huge challenge playing Toulouse in their own stadium would be. Toulouse started really quickly and we were struggling to get our hands on the ball. At the end of the first half, Toulouse were 24 points to 10 up after scoring three tries. We'd scored a try (created by me winning one against the head at a scrum) through Dafydd James – such a great try scorer in Europe – in one of the rare times we managed to go through some phases, but going in at half-time we knew we had to do better. At half-time Phil stressed to us that there would be opportunities: we just had to stay patient and believe in ourselves. Early in the second half, Poitrenaud scored a try which was converted, giving them a 21 point lead – a points difference they had twice in the second half. Things looked bleak, but then we started gaining possession and creating our own chances. We scored two tries in a crazy three-minute period – Alix Popham chipped over the top and regathered (a trick I'd never even seen him practise), before releasing Darren Daniel to race in for the first try. The second was following a searing break from Dwayne who freed Barry Davies to run in for the try. Stephen Jones converted both and suddenly from nowhere we were only 4 points behind, with the scoreboard showing 31 points to 27. Toulouse then kicked a penalty to extend their lead, only for Daniel to touch down again with Stephen converting. It was now neck and neck: game on.

With only a few minutes remaining, Toulouse's Irishman Trevor Brennan was held up over the line by Darren Daniel in a great bit of defensive work. We slowly worked our way back down the field, driving the ball up, looking either for a penalty for any indiscretions from Toulouse or to get Stephen into a drop goal position. We still seemed too far out but the ball went back to Stephen to take on what looked like an unlikely drop goal from the halfway line – however, Toulouse anticipated this and moved up quickly. Stephen, showing his class, made a swift decision that the drop goal wasn't on and offloaded to Regan King, never a bad move to make. The centre yet again showed his brilliance at evading tackles and took the ball to within five metres of the line. Regan was then tackled, but popped up a beautiful pass for replacement Nathan Thomas, who was there in support, to dive over the line. We couldn't believe it – we were in raptures. Luckily, Stephen was the calmest man out there and slotted over the conversion. We'd gone to Toulouse and defeated them, completing the double over them. It was a fantastic achievement. The players and the fans were going wild – such an occasion. I think it's safe to say we drank a fair bit on the journey back from France, and all carried on our celebrations in Cardiff city centre. Great memories.

In the final two pool matches, we defeated Ulster away in a convincing manner and managed a narrow victory at home to London Irish. We were undefeated in a pool – at the time only the fifth team in the history of the tournament to achieve that. We dominated the pool so decisively that only one team qualified from our pool that year – testimony to the number of points we took off the other sides.

We were now in the quarter-finals, where our opponents would be the reigning European Champions, Munster. Phil had organised a break at St Brides in Saundersfoot, so we all went down for a few days to relax and for a change of scenery (with a couple of rugby sessions thrown in), as a way of treating us before a big game. Due to how well we'd qualified, we secured a home draw at Stradey Park and the game was a sell-out. Munster had stars such as Christian Cullen, O'Gara, Stringer, Horan, Quinlan, Wallace and Leamy, but they were missing Paul O'Connell, a real talisman for them. We started the game really quickly and got out into a 17-0 lead with tries from Dafydd James and Gavin Thomas – both converted by Stephen Jones – and Barry Davies also bagged a long-range penalty. Our forwards were really carrying strongly and Alix Popham in particular was causing them major problems. When in this form, Alix was a real handful for any defence in Europe at that time. Munster started to get back in the game and when replacement Inoke Afeaki, who was outstanding that season for us, was sin-binned, Munster made the most of their one-man advantage with their winger Dowling scoring a try. However, still with a man down, we also managed to score a decisive try. Regan King, yet again brilliant, put Mark Jones away and Mark passed on to Scott MacLeod, who produced a great pass around the defender to put Barry over for the try. Stephen nailed the conversion and we'd done it: we'd knocked out the reigning Champions amidst great scenes at Stradey Park. We'd be in the semi-finals.

Our opponents in the semi-final would be Leicester Tigers, with the game being played at the Walkers Stadium, the home of Leicester City FC. Obviously, confidence was high given that we were so far undefeated and after beating a very strong Munster team, but we didn't underestimate the Leicester side. Leicester played very well, with Andy Goode at 10 in particular having a great game. Goode scored the opening try and a total of 18 points in the match. We had our moments, scoring two tries through Mark Jones and yours truly, and did lead briefly, but on the day Leicester were the better side and further tries from Shane Jennings and Louis Deacon secured them a spot in the final. It goes without saying how disappointed we were to have fallen at the semi-final stage, but we'd shown Europe how good we could be. If we could strengthen the squad, with finances coming in from a new stadium and some backing from the board, then who knows: perhaps next season we could be back at these stages again, and hopefully get even further.

CHAPTER 5

The Boy from Ton Plays for Wales

As MENTIONED IN a previous chapter, I was unfortunate to miss out on a Welsh call-up whilst with Celtic Warriors due to injury and the number of good Welsh hookers playing at that time, such as Mefin Davies, Robin McBryde, Gareth Williams, T R 'Rhys' Thomas, Huw Bennett and Richard Hibbard. I had my work cut out to achieve my dream – playing for my country.

Finally, after a season with Scarlets, I had my opportunity. Wales were touring that summer to North America to play against USA and Canada, and I was delighted to be named in the squad selected. I was one of three hookers named, the others being T R Thomas and my old mate, Mef. Earlier that year, Wales had won the Six Nations Grand Slam under coach Mike Ruddock, and a number of players who'd helped Wales to victory were unavailable for this tour. This gave promising but inexperienced players such as Ben Broster, Chris Czekaj, Matthew Jones, Richie Pugh, Tal Selley and me – none of whom had appeared in previous squads – an opportunity to show what we could do. I was determined I was going to make the most of this chance.

The tour was just two Test matches: firstly USA and then Canada. Mefin was struggling with an injury, and it was clear in the early training sessions that he wasn't going to be ready to play against USA, which meant for the first game there was a straight shoot-out between me and TR. At the time, neither of us had played for our country and we were both battling to change that. TR's a year or so younger than me and was a quality player I'd had many battles with when playing for our respective regions. The question was, who'd get the nod? When the team was announced I was elated: playing for Wales wearing the number 2 shirt would be Matthew Rees. The boy from Tonyrefail was going to represent his country. I was the first and am still the only lad born in Tonyrefail to play for Wales. Rugby legend Cliff Morgan was the first Wales player who went to Tonyrefail Comprehensive, but he was born in Trebanog, a nearby village. Being the first player born in Tonyrefail to win a Wales cap is something I'm very proud of. My family and loved ones were delighted when I contacted them to tell them the news. Unfortunately, they weren't there to see the match in person, but they watched it from home, proud to see me playing for Wales.

East Hartford, Connecticut, 4th June 2005: a moment that will remain with me forever. As I walked out in the famous red shirt, a wave of emotions came over me. I was remembering my schooldays, my friends and family, and also during the national anthem looked up and in the crowd saw Mefin Davies, a man who'd been there throughout my career, which made me feel very proud. It was a bright sunny day, great for playing running rugby. Captain was Mark Taylor, who was captaining his country for the first time. We had a very changed team from the 2005 Grand Slam side, with ten players being away on British and Irish Lions duty in New Zealand – including my old mate Melon, the first of three tours he'd take part in. We still had experience in the side, with people such as Rhys Williams, Jamie Robinson, Ian Gough and Colin Charvis. The USA started the game quickly, and only good defence by us kept them out. Shortly after that Ceri Sweeney, playing at inside centre, went over for our first try. At the end of the first half we'd scored six tries in total: in addition to Ceri's, Craig

Morgan, Nicky Robinson, Kevin Morgan, Jonathan Thomas and Rhys Williams all crossed the whitewash. We led 42 points to 3 – I loved international rugby!

In the second half, as per the first, we played some really good rugby and scored more tries. The second half saw a number of changes and I was replaced by TR after 50 minutes. I was pleased to get 50 minutes and was happy with my performance but I knew there was plenty to work on to get to where I needed to be. However, overall it was a good start to international rugby. Tal Selley and Richie Pugh also came on to make their debuts and also got on the scoresheet with tries. Colin Charvis, one of the most experienced playing that day for Wales, scored two tries and had a great game. The final score was USA 3 Wales 77. I'd finally made my debut, and I was determined it wasn't going to be my last outing for the national side. As it was an experimental tour, the following week for the game against Canada they went with TR starting and with Mef now fit, he'd be on the bench. Naturally I was disappointed, but I could understand that Mike wanted to give game time to as many players as possible on the tour.

The match was played in Toronto and Wales got another convincing victory, by 60 points to 3. Ben Broster and TR both scored on their first start for Wales and Chris Czekaj scored on his debut with a stunning 60 m try. A number of players got an opportunity on this tour to play for their country and show the coaches what they could do. The standard of opposition wasn't as high as it could have been, but it was a fantastic experience for us all and didn't diminish the fact that I was playing for my country. Ryan Jones, who'd started against the USA at 8, wasn't available to us for the Canada game as he'd been called up to replace the injured Simon Taylor for the British and Irish Lions in New Zealand. Ryan did very well and even though he'd been called up late and was relatively inexperienced at international level, he went on to play in all three Test matches, starting the last two. He came away from the tour with a much bigger reputation, which not many Lions did on that tour. He certainly made the most of his opportunity. I wasn't selected for the 2005 Autumn Series – Mike Ruddock phoned me to let me know it had been a close call and that I just needed to keep on working hard on my game. I was disappointed not to be selected, but reassured that I just needed to knuckle down and concentrate on my game.

The 2006 Six Nations soon came around, and Mike picked Mef and TR as the two hookers for the squad. It must have been close, but I missed out on a squad place. From a Welsh perspective, the tournament is remembered for the resignation of Mike Ruddock only two games in, with Scott Johnson taking over on an interim basis. There have been a lot of stories surrounding Mike leaving his position as Wales Coach. I wasn't around the squads enough to form a personal view of my own, but I do know that other players felt that his involvement in the coaching wasn't what it should have been, with Scott and some of the senior players taking the majority of the sessions. In the Six Nations that year, Wales only won against Scotland, drew against Italy and lost the other games, including substantial losses to England and Ireland. As Grand Slam winners the year before, this was a huge disappointment. Over the campaign, TR had established himself as the first-choice hooker, with Mef as the back-up. I had a big challenge on my hands to get back into the squad, but having tasted international rugby, I wanted more.

In April 2006, Gareth Jenkins was named as the new Welsh coach. From a selfish perspective, I thought this might well be good for my international career. I had been Gareth's first-choice hooker at the Scarlets, so I was really optimistic that this could propel me into the upcoming Welsh squads and was looking to build on my solitary cap from the previous summer. I also was aware that there was a summer tour coming up to Argentina with Wales. When the squad was announced, I was one of three hookers named for the tour, alongside Huw Bennett and Richard Hibbard. I was delighted to be back in the Welsh fold.

The first Test was played in Puerto Madryn, where there's a community of people of Welsh descent. I was selected and alongside me in the front row were two Ospreys: Duncan Jones – who captained the side – and Adam Jones, aka the 'hair bear bunch'. Making their debuts for Wales that day were a young-looking Alun Wyn Jones, who started at 6, and also Ian Evans, who started at lock. Ianto was a real character, and great around the squad even in those early days. Argentina that day had a very strong side out – all very experienced players who deserved all the credit they were given, with Juan Martín Hernández at 15, Felipe Contepomi at 12, Agustín Pichot (who was captain) at 9, Juan Martín Fernández Lobbe at 7 and a fantastic front row of Martín Scelzo, Mario Ledesma and Rodrigo Roncero – all outstanding players.

The game was very close and we scored three tries, the first a great one through Ianto, who intercepted a pass just inside our half. He showed a turn of pace which surprised the Argentinians, but his teammates even more! We had no idea he could move that quickly. James Hook, who came off the bench to make his debut, and Mark Jones also got on the scoresheet. In the second half I was replaced by Richard Hibbard, who became the fourth person to make their debut in that match. Argentina also scored three tries that day and just edged over the line with a win by a scoreline of 27 points to 25. When I look back, a two-point loss against that Argentinian side wasn't that bad a result, but a defeat is a defeat.

Before the second Test in Buenos Aires, Gareth told me that he wanted to give Huw Bennett the start for this match, with Richard Hibbard on the bench. He said that he was pleased with my performance in the first Test, but after hearing those words there was a part of me wondering if I'd have another long wait before I got back into the national squad, like after being left out of the second game of the North American tour. The game itself was a really tough one for us. Argentina were very good on the day – much better than in the first Test. We did score three tries through Lee Byrne, Gareth Delve and Shane

Williams, but lost by a scoreline of 45 points to 27. In terms of my performance in the one game I played, I felt I'd done well but I'd have to wait for Wales' next lot of games to see if I'd be called up again. These would be the Autumn Internationals against Australia, Pacific Islands, Canada and New Zealand. Until then, all I could do was start the season well with the Scarlets and hope that my form would be good enough to get me into the squad.

Fortunately for me, the 2006–07 season started well for the Scarlets and me. By the time the Welsh squad was announced for the Autumn Series, we'd made a good start in the Heineken Cup, beating London Irish and Ulster, and I was in good form. I was named in the national squad alongside two others in my position, TR Thomas and Huw Bennett. Mef at that time was into his second season with Gloucester, so release to play for his country was proving a sticking point – as it was then and still is now for players who play outside Wales. At that point both of my two caps had been won on foreign soil, so having the chance to play in Wales in front of family and friends in the Millennium Stadium in Cardiff was huge.

First game up, as mentioned, was Australia. I was fortunate enough to be given the starting number 2 shirt and I'd be packing down in the front row between Melon and Adam 'Bomb' Jones – a front row that it was my pleasure to be part of for my country many times over the future years. For my first home international at the Millennium Stadium, that great rugby theatre was packed with over 74,000 enthusiastic fans. Australia had some star names in their ranks including Stephen Larkham, Chris Latham, Phil Waugh and Matt Giteau – who on that day played at 9, and in a role foreign to him was absolutely outstanding, just showing the quality of the player. We had a really good side out ourselves, including Alfie, Shane Williams, Gavin Henson, Dwayne Peel and captain Stephen Jones. We suffered an early blow after only 25 minutes, with Stephen having to go off due to an injury, and being replaced by James Hook. At the point Hooky came on, we were already down by 17 points to 6 after three quick tries from Australia, with Giteau orchestrating things beautifully and scoring one himself from a tap penalty, when he caught us all napping. We managed to score a try via Shane and went in at half-time only one point behind, which, after the way Australia had been playing, was a real positive for us.

In the match we had a dominant scrum throughout the game – we were getting a real shove on, both on our ball and theirs – and it was no surprise when they brought on grizzled veteran Brendan Cannon for Tai McIsaac for the second half at hooker (bit of a victory for me, that one; when they have to replace your opposite number). For a novice international at that point, Hooky was playing really well and kicking beautifully, and we got another try through Martyn Williams, which Hooky converted. Australia then scored a try (Cameron Shepherd's second) and there was a brilliant bit of individual play from full back Chris Latham, who took a kick downfield from Kevin Morgan, evading tackles and showing great pace down the touchline to score a great try. Hooky later kicked a penalty following another strong scrum by us which they were for penalised for collapsing, and the game was tied. The game ebbed and flowed and for the last five minutes we were under real pressure, but managed to keep them out to draw the game. The first ever drawn game in history between the two sides. A draw against a very good Southern Hemisphere side wasn't the worst start to an Autumn Series.

The following week Wales played the Pacific Islanders, a side made up of players from Samoa, Fiji and Tonga, three passionate rugby-playing countries coming together due to the financial constraints each country had individually when it came to touring costs. Wales made a few changes from the week before and these included TR getting the start at hooker, with Huw Bennett on the bench. Wales won the game by 38 points to 20, scoring five tries – all converted by Ceri Sweeney, who got the start at 10. Playing for the Pacific Islanders that day was my old mate from my Celtic Warrior days, Maama

Molitika, who was an early replacement. It was brilliant to catch up with him afterwards – a great man.

The third match of the Autumn Series was against Canada. I'd missed out on playing against them the year before on the North American tour but wouldn't this time. I was starting, with TR on the bench. The following week we were going to be playing New Zealand, and I was wondering if me playing against Canada meant I'd miss out for that encounter, so I was eager to put up a strong showing to give Gareth a decision to make when it came to selection against the All Blacks.

The game went well for me personally and for Wales. We won 61 points to 26 and scored nine tries in total, including my first ever international try. It was in the left-hand corner after a break from my Llanelli Scarlets teammate Dwayne Peel, who then popped me the pass to finish from around 10 metres out. A fantastic feeling: a try for Wales in Cardiff in front of my family. I came off after 52 minutes to be replaced by TR, but I was happy with how I'd done, especially scoring a try. I'd just have to wait and see if I'd done enough to get the spot to play against the All Blacks.

In the build-up, training certainly turned up a notch, as we were all desperate to play against the All Blacks. When Gareth announced the side, I was disappointed to find out I'd be on the bench, with TR getting the start. Even before the kick-off there was controversy, as New Zealand completed their Haka in the changing room due to a disagreement over being asked by the WRU to complete their traditional war dance after their national anthem but before our anthem. It certainly seemed to fire up the New Zealanders even more, and it was a real disappointment for the players that we couldn't accept their challenge on the pitch and for the fans not to see it. They scored a try after only four minutes via Luke McAlister and before the break, Sitiveni Sivivatu had scored two more. The winger was unstoppable that day with his pace and power, and with players such as Dan Carter feeding him, we couldn't get near him. I came on with around eight minutes left but the game was long over as a competition by then. We did score a try via Martyn Williams, but the final scoreline was a defeat by 45 points to 10. New Zealand had played at another level of speed, skill and intensity to us, and we all knew we had a lot of hard work ahead of us.

The 2007 Six Nations was Gareth's first as coach and was also my first participation in this great tournament, and I was really looking forward to it. The first opponents would be Ireland in Cardiff, and when it came to the selection of our side, Gareth had a number of injuries and Alfie being suspended to contend with. Chris Czekaj replaced Alfie and we had Hal Luscombe – primarily a centre by trade – on the other wing. We also had an inexperienced pairing in midfield in Jamie Robinson and James Hook. In the front row, the selection was Melon, TR and Chris Horsman. I had to make do with a place on the bench. After only 30-odd seconds, Ronan O'Gara put up a kick on Czekaj and he, instead of clearing the ball into touch or downfield, put a pass infield to skipper Stephen Jones. Stephen hurriedly tried to clear the ball but Brian O'Driscoll was up very quickly to charge down the clearance, and Rory Best was able to gather up the ball to score the try after only 46 seconds. O'Driscoll scored another try before the break, but three penalties from Stephen had us right in the game. Unfortunately, we didn't score at all in the second half, and a further try from Denis Leamy gave them the victory by 19 points to 9. I came on after 67 minutes, replacing TR, for my first taste of Six Nations rugby – which was a thrill even though it ended in defeat.

The following weekend we were at Murrayfield to take on the Scots. Gareth made a few changes, including two in the front row with Duncan Jones and Adam Jones coming in for Melon and Chris Horsman, but TR retained the number 2 shirt and I was on the bench again. The game was one to be forgotten: both teams were below average, but particularly us. Scotland won with seven Chris Paterson penalties to three Stephen Jones penalties, no tries scored by either side. The

Welsh fans that had travelled up weren't backward in making their feelings known as we left the field. I played the last 20 minutes in a game that was of a very poor standard. Gareth was under pressure, as were the players: we needed to turn this around. But it would be tough – next up two weeks later would be the French in Paris, and they were undefeated so far in this Championship.

In front of 80,000 fans in Stade de France, I finally got the start at hooker in a game that was really exciting to play in. We started really well, getting two early tries through Alix Popham and Tom Shanklin and were playing some good stuff. France came back later in the first half with tries of their own from Christophe Dominici and Lionel Nallet and with solid goal-kicking from David Skrela, leading at half-time by 23 points to 14. Early in the second half, Shanklin was stopped just short of the try line after a great counter attack as we continued to cause them problems, but unfortunately both Stephen and Hooky missed a few kicks which could have got us even closer. I was replaced by TR on 72 minutes and a few minutes later Jamie Robinson scored a great try under the posts. Unfortunately, it wasn't enough and France ran out 32 points to 21 winners and continued their undefeated run. We'd played a lot better than the previous week and looked dangerous with the ball in hand, but a loss is still a loss, and to come away with no points in a close game was frustrating for all. Three games into the Championship and three defeats – not the result I or anyone else in Wales wanted.

Next up was Italy in Rome. The Italians in their last outing had earned their first ever away victory in the Six Nations. I got the start and we all knew we had to get going quickly and try to destroy the obvious confidence the win over Scotland would carry into this game for the Italians. In the opening minutes we had a narrow escape: a great break from the centre Gonzalo Canale cut us open but his long pass out to their winger was forward and the try was chalked off. We then scored a try through Shane Williams after a great inside pass from Tom

Shanklin. Italy scored through winger Kaine Robertson to lead 13 points to 7 at half-time. I then scored a try off a line-out – I peeled around the back, took the ball and handed off Alessandro Troncon after my break, and a dummy opened the way for me to score under the posts. I was pretty pleased, to say the least. Ultimately though, the game will be remembered for the incident at the end when referee Chris White gave us a penalty inside the Italy half. At the time we were down by three points, so we asked the referee if we had time to kick to touch to go for the line-out and attempt a try to get the victory. Receiving an answer in the affirmative, Hooky kicked to touch, but as soon as he had, the referee blew up for full time. We couldn't believe it – we'd lost, but felt rightly aggrieved. If we'd known there was no time when awarded the penalty, Hooky would have taken the three points and the draw. All the talk over this incident, though, did paint over the fact that it was another defeat and another poor performance overall. We hadn't won a game in the whole Championship, and were looking at finishing bottom and getting the wooden spoon. Last up was England in Cardiff, and we needed a win desperately – beating England was all we had left in this tournament.

England came into this game still with a slim chance of winning the Championship. They'd lost to Ireland but had won all their other games, so if France lost to Scotland in Paris, then there was a small opportunity. However, we were determined that no such mathematics would be necessary. The match itself was in front of 74,500 fans, the large majority Welsh and baying for a Welsh victory. We had to deliver one for them, after a really poor tournament.

I was selected to start. We had a good side out, with Alfie back after suspension and slotting in at centre alongside Tom Shanklin, and a back three of Kevin Morgan, Mark Jones and Shane Williams. Stephen Jones was out, so in came James Hook to play at 10 with Dwayne at 9. The front row was made up of Melon, Chris Horsman and me, the second row of Ian Gough and Alun Wyn and the back row of Alix Popham, Ryan

Jones and Martyn Williams. England coached by Brian Ashton had a decent side as well, with players like Mark Cueto, Mike Catt, Jason Robinson, Joe Worsley, James Haskell and Tom Rees in their ranks.

The game started really well for us and we scored a try after two minutes, when Hooky charged down an attempted clearance kick from Toby Flood close to the England line, and regathered to score. Only moments later we almost scored again but were held up just short, but then shortly after that Horsman scored a try after a great break by Melon. We were rampant, playing great stuff and the noise in the stadium was fantastic. We were going really well, but then a bit of magic from Mike Catt in the centre opened us up, and his pass to Harry Ellis had the scrum half scampering in for the try – that moment of magic had put them back in the game. A few penalties from Flood and Hooky had the score at 18 points to 10 in our favour, only for a breakdown in communication in our defence to give Ellis the opportunity to get away from a ruck, and his offload to Robinson got the outstanding winger in at the corner. We went in at half-time 18-15 up. After playing a great first half, they were only three points down, which was pretty disappointing, but we knew we were playing better rugby. We had to tighten up in defence and take our chances when they came. We were lucky there was no punishment when Horsman kicked Joe Worsley in the head – nowadays that would be a red card, a lengthy ban and a hefty fine.

Early in the second half Catt had to be replaced due to injury, which was certainly a blow to them, and from then on, we dominated the game. Hooky was outstanding at 10, playing well in his passing game and his kicking game was outstanding. He nailed a few penalties – one a long-range effort – as well as an outstanding drop goal. He finished the game with 22 points in our 27 to 18 victory. I played the whole game and was really pleased with how the set pieces went, as well as my overall contribution elsewhere. Due to the win and Scotland losing heavily in France, it was Scotland that finished bottom of the table, not us, with France winning the Grand Slam. It was still a hugely disappointing tournament, but beating England and not finishing bottom gave us something small to hold onto. Personally speaking, I'd played the last three matches ahead of TR, and was hoping that I was now securing a place in at least the squad, but I so wanted to be the number-one choice for Wales at hooker. There was a summer tour to Australia coming up and then a World Cup, which I was desperate to be at. I'd missed out on the 2003 World Cup, and was determined to do all I could not to miss this one.

CHAPTER 6

Rugby World Cup 2007 – Gareth Jenkins' Last Stand

FOLLOWING ON FROM our win in the final Six Nations game against England, a very good win against a team who at the end of the same year got to a World Cup Final, the Welsh squad and coaches felt we were in decent shape going into our summer tour to Australia. However, the plan was for me not to be touring. My wife Becky was heavily pregnant and with the tour in late May and Becky due in early June 2007, I'd told Gareth Jenkins that I'd have to miss it. I'd just had a run of games as the starting hooker, but if missing the tour impacted on whether or not I'd be going into the World Cup that summer, then so be it – I was determined not to miss the birth of my child.

Before the squad was announced for the two-match tour – Tests against Australia in Sydney and Brisbane – a few players were ruled out through injury and a few senior established players were left at home after a long season to rest up for the upcoming World Cup. In the front five positions, there was a real shortage of available players. Because of this, Gareth Jenkins got in contact with me, asking if I could please reconsider. Mef wasn't going to be fit for the first Test, TR wasn't available, and Gareth didn't feel Richard Hibbard was quite ready to start. As I'd already explained the situation with my wife in the very late stages of pregnancy, Gareth suggested that I could come out just for the first Test and that they'd then fly me straight back afterwards. Mef would be ready for the second Test; he just needed me to be there for the first one. Obviously, I had to discuss this with Becky. She said she was comfortable that if I was only going to be there for the build-up to the first Test and could then fly back, she was happy for me to go. I'd be going to Oz on a summer tour with Wales after all.

As you all know, the flight to Australia's a long old trip from the UK. When we got there, just over a week before the first Test, the lads were looking forward to a bit of a rest, maybe a few massage sessions and then starting the training to get ready for the upcoming Test match. When we got to the hotel, we went to our rooms and then met in the hotel reception. Players had a recovery session (split into forwards and backs) and then whilst in the pool, Gareth advised that recovery protocol was to have a few beers in the hotel. The few beers just kept coming and coming and as there was a nightclub under the premises, you've probably guessed that the recuperation continued there until the early hours.

The morning after the night before, there were some training drills run, with some players really struggling to complete those simple activities due to dehydration. Gareth Jenkins then decided that those simple warm-up exercises were enough for now and that we were going for a few drinks. And as with the night before, the few drinks went on for many hours. Many of us were looking at each other and asking 'What's going on?' Yes, there was still over a week to the first international, but for two days we'd pretty much been solidly on the booze!

The following day was a Saturday, and Gareth Jenkins and Alan Phillips, Wales Team Manager, had organised a day trip to Sydney. That evening there was going to be a formal function that the players and coaches had been asked to attend. Shortly after we got on the coach to travel to Sydney, Gareth Jenkins got on the mic at the front of the coach. He announced to the group that we were going to have a great day out, with plenty of singing but no spewing! When we got to Sydney, the players and management team went off in small groups to different places, including a few bars, etc. – I'm sure you get the picture. Later on at the function, all the players and a few of the coaches were there, but Gareth Jenkins was nowhere to be seen. This was a bit embarrassing for the players and in particular the tour Captain, Alfie.

When we came down the following day for breakfast, Alfie spoke privately to Alan Phillips on behalf of the players and said that we needed some control putting in place, that the last few days had been crazy for an international side playing in a Test match one week later, and that Australia could humiliate us if we didn't take it seriously. Those words were listened to and for the rest of the week, training was far more organised and serious. When the side was selected, I was indeed starting at 2 with Hibbs on the bench. The side was decent with Lee Byrne, Alfie and Czekaj in the back three, a midfield of Jamie Robinson and Sonny Parker, and Hooky and Mike Phillips as the half-backs. The front row consisted of Iestyn Thomas, myself and Adam Jones, the second row of Brent Cockbain and Robert Sidoli, and the back row of Colin Charvis, Gavin Thomas and Jonathan Thomas. Australia had players such as Stirling Mortlock, Adam Ashley-Cooper, Matt Giteau, Nathan Sharpe, Rocky Elsom and Phil Waugh: a very talented side.

The Stadium Australia's a very impressive place to play. Running out that day, there was a part of me wondering what was going to happen and hoping that Becky wouldn't be having the baby before I got home to Wales. The Aussies had a late change in their side: Stephen Larkham, their very talented number 10, was injured and was replaced by Sam Norton-Knight, a player that many in Wales and in particular Cardiff Blues will know. A player who it's fair to say really struggled in the 10 position two years later in the Celtic League, was starting for his country against us in that same position.

Early in the match, Norton-Knight threw out a poor pass to Mortlock which went behind the player. Mortlock dropped it, allowing Czekaj to pick up the ball and kick ahead, Hooky regathered the ball and fed Alfie, who showed great strength to hold off tackles and carry a few of the opposition over the line with him. Alfie was making his 93rd appearance on that day, and that try was his 38th try for Wales, both new Welsh records by the hugely talented player.

Australian full back Julian Huxley then threw an interception pass to Jamie Robinson, who galloped away to score another try, both tries converted by Hooky. Hooky also kicked a penalty after Byrney was tackled by Mark Gerrard just short of the try line, and when we tried to secure the ball on the floor, Australia were penalised by South African referee Jonathan Kaplan. We were 17-0 up against Australia! Australia started to get some decent possession and after a few phases, Aussie number 8 Wycliff Palu barged over the line. A bit later on, Nathan Sharpe also scored a try, converted by Mortlock. Going in at half-time we were leading 17 points to 12.

The second half got underway and we were in the Aussie half, really putting their defence to work. We finally got a penalty that Hooky slotted over – a good start to the second half. Australia were a classy side with talented players; none more so than Matt Giteau. After we turned the ball over, Giteau showed a great piece of individual skill by dummying past a few defenders to score a try. Mortlock kicked the conversion and then kicked a penalty after an indiscretion by us, putting Australia in the lead for the first time in the whole game. We needed a response, and after a few carries by the forwards, we were awarded a penalty that Hooky unfortunately missed. Shortly afterwards, Charvis carried strongly and when the ball came back to Hooky he calmly dropped a goal. We were back in front 23 points to 22, and time was running out for the Aussies.

With less than ten minutes to go, we made a few changes. I came off to be replaced by Hibbs, and one of the other changes was Mike Phillips being replaced by Gareth Cooper. Australia kept pushing for a breakthrough but we were defending well.

When we got possession back, the lads tried to play a sensible game and not take any chances. The clock was ticking down – we were almost there, and we had possession. Gareth Cooper received the ball: his plan was to put it off the park as time had almost elapsed. However, the ball stayed in play and was collected by Huxley, who brought the ball back, making great yards. Our defence was scampering to get back into position, in one last defensive stand as Australia moved the attack from one side of the pitch to the other. George Smith, who'd come on as a replacement for Waugh, threw out a long pass which Hooky desperately tried to intercept to no avail, and it landed in the arms of Stephen Hoiles, also an earlier replacement for Palu, who went in for the winning try. Mortlock kicked the conversion, which meant the final score was Australia 29, Wales 23. We were devastated, especially Coops after his attempted clearance kick failed to find touch. We'd come so close to our first victory in Australia since 1969 – after a few days on the booze, maybe Gareth Jenkins was onto something with his preparation!

As promised by Gareth and the WRU, I was flown home after the game and thankfully arrived with plenty of time to be by Becky's side to see the birth of my daughter Brooke. It was a life-changing moment. The following weekend I sat down at home in Tonyrefail to watch the second Test with my wife and daughter, and what a huge difference from the first Test it was! Bar a few changes, including Mef starting at hooker, it was pretty much the same Welsh side that had taken the field a week earlier. Australia were very similar too, but on the day were streets ahead of us. The Aussies scored three tries without a response from us, eventually running out 31 points to nil victors. The game is most remembered for the horrific injury Chris Czekaj picked up. The winger shattered his femur in five places and was out for over a year recovering. It was a terrible blow for a young man who'd only just started his international career, and he was never the same player again. That day was also the one on which Mef played his last international for

Wales, although he played for another five years for Leicester Tigers and Ospreys to round off a fabulous career. This was the man who'd taken me under his wing all those years before at Pontypridd, and had taught me so much about my position. A top man. I owe him a lot – thanks Mef, for all your assistance.

The World Cup was now a few months away, so those hoping or expecting to be part of the Wales squad had some recovery time to get ready. Some pre-tournament warm-up games had been arranged prior to travelling to France. We were going to play England at Twickenham, and then two home games against Argentina and France. The Wales coaches announced an extended squad for the training camp prior to the England game and then the plan was to announce the squad which would be going to France for the World Cup after that match. The Wales management decided for the England game to rest a few of the first-teamers to give a few fringe players the opportunity to either break into the World Cup squad or cement their position within it. But it was still a decent side: Byrney, Shanks, Alfie, Dafydd James, AWJ and Charvis all started, but the match was painful to watch. England absolutely blitzed us, scoring nine tries in the process, with England number 8 Nick Easter scoring four of them. England, reigning World Champions going into the tournament, were now full of confidence, while ours would have to be scraped up off the floor. Gareth Jenkins took a lot of criticism in the national papers on his selection for the game, and as players, we now had two games prior to the start of the World Cup to get us back up and running again.

The following weekend the 30-man World Cup squad was announced. Alfie would be captain, with two vice-captains named in Dwayne Peel and Stephen Jones. And named as one of the three hookers selected, alongside Huw Bennett and T R Thomas, was Matthew Rees – I was elated. I was going to my first ever World Cup. I'd always wondered if I hadn't been unable to tour due to injury just before the World Cup in 2003 whether I could have forced my way into contention then, but now I was in on merit. It was a great feeling. We felt we had a good squad, with a number of players still around from the 2005 Grand Slam squad, plus a few lads who'd been part of the Wales U21 Grand Slam 2003 side. There was a good blend of youth and experience and in the pool we were in – Pool B with Australia, Canada, Fiji and Japan, with games in France and in Cardiff – we felt we had a great chance to progress far in the tournament. However, after the squad was announced, we had to concentrate on the two upcoming matches to get us in a good positive frame of mind and get a run of wins together.

The game against Argentina was a strange affair, and the atmosphere was subdued throughout. Obviously, the group were under pressure after the English hammering, and confidence wasn't helped when Argentina scored the first try after an interception. However, we came back and played some decent stuff. Alfie scored a try early on, as did Alun Wyn, who was outstanding that day, as he so often is. AWJ was back at his best position at lock (rather than 6, which he'd played two weeks earlier), and it showed. Mark Jones also scored a try in the first half, so we went into the break 24 points to 7 to the good. Unfortunately, tactically we were poor in the second half and allowed Argentina back into the game. The Pumas had a huge amount of possession, and were taking their chances. With ten minutes left, they were only 7 points behind us, and I was sin-binned after yet more pressure put on us, with their forwards really putting us to the cosh. At the end, they'd have scored a try if it hadn't been for a great defensive effort by Duncan Jones. We held on for the win, but it wasn't a great performance.

France were next up. The French would be hosting the upcoming tournament, and after their Grand Slam exploits earlier that year were one of the favourites to win the World Cup. They came to Cardiff with a fine side selected, including Rougerie, Jauzion, Clerc, Betsen, Harinordoquy and a front row of De Villiers, Szarzewski and Mas. I started, and the French were very good on the day, strong in the forwards and the backs caused us no end of issues. The French had already

67

beaten England twice in their warm-up games and were too good for us in this one. They scored four tries, with Hooky scoring our only one. The final score was 34 points to 7 to France. The warm-up games had been a real lesson to us: we still believed we had the players to be serious contenders in the pool, but our form wasn't right. We were determined to find that form in France for the World Cup. It was all about peaking at the right time, and that time was almost upon us.

The 2007 World Cup was to be played mainly in France, but there'd also be games played in Cardiff and in Edinburgh. We'd get to play two of our pool games in Cardiff against Australia and Japan, and the other two matches in Nantes against Canada and Fiji. Australia had been the World Champions before England. We'd played them a number of times in recent years and had toured there only a few months earlier – they were good but we felt we could cause an upset. We knew the other teams in the pool would give it their all – they were proud players playing for their country in a World Cup – but we all felt we could get to the knock-out stages and then after that, who knows?

Our first game in the tournament would be against Canada in the Stade de la Beaujoire, Nantes. Our French base for the tournament was a hotel just outside Nantes. Training was going well and the coaching team were busy making a decision on team selection for the first game. In terms of where we were staying, the hotel was fine, but it was situated out in the middle of nowhere. The boys used to go down the road to the only café for a coffee in between training sessions. It was a bit too quiet for my liking: we'd be there for a few weeks and needed something to occupy us, but maybe the WRU had learnt their lesson after the tour to Australia only a few months earlier with the first few days on the booze.

When the team was announced for the first game, there was a bit of a shock for many. Alfie, who was our captain and had been playing really well in the lead-up to the World Cup, wasn't selected. Sonny Parker came into the centre alongside Shanks.

Hooky was selected over Stephen Jones, who'd been injured but was now fit. I was selected in the front row alongside Melon and Adam 'Bomb' Jones. Alfie and Stephen were down as replacements, but it was a surprise that the captain and one of his vice-captains would start the World Cup on the bench. Captaining the side for the first game would be Dwayne Peel. Peely had been named as one of the vice-captains for the World Cup and now in the first game up would captain his country for the first time: a massive honour. I'm sure that Canada looked at our team selection and surmised that we felt that even without Alfie and Stephen Jones, we had enough to beat them. Those in their team such as Rod Snow, Jon Thiel and Jamie Cudmore were passionate, proud players, well known to rugby fans, and they'd try and use them to fire up their whole team. As players, we had to ensure Gareth Jenkins' selection didn't backfire on us all.

The game was played on a bright sunny day in Nantes. We wore a new grey kit on the day, with black armbands in honour of the passing of Sir Tasker Watkins, a huge influence in Welsh rugby. We went 9 points to 0 up following three penalties from Hooky inside fifteen minutes and all seemed fine – how wrong we were. Canada had a big, heavy pack of forwards and started to put us under serious pressure. Not long after that, Cudmore forced himself over the line to score a try. Ten minutes later, Craig Culpan, the Canadian centre, picked off a pass from Hooky when we were on the attack and looking destined to score, and ran almost the full length of the pitch to score another try. We went in at half-time 12 points to 9 down. Their pack and scrum half Morgan Williams were running the show. The pressure was really on.

Just five minutes into the second half, Canada scored again, Williams getting over the line after their forwards had again carried the ball very strongly. Straight after the conversion was missed, Gareth Jenkins brought on Alfie and Stephen Jones for Kevin Morgan and Hooky. We needed to get back into this match, and turned to two experienced internationals to help us do that – two players who many people had wanted to start the game. Instantly Stephen almost scored a try himself, just being held up over the line. Minutes later a reverse pass from Stephen put Sonny Parker over for the score. Five minutes later, we got back into the lead when a clearance kick from Canada was charged down, and Alun Wyn gathered up the ball in his big mitts to score the try. Shane then scored two tries and Colin Charvis (also a replacement) scored another, with the Canadians seriously tiring in the second half. The final score was Wales 42 Canada 17. The scoreline now looks like a straightforward victory but it was far from it. In the first half we were in real trouble and if it hadn't been for a big improvement in the second half, with a few changes in personnel and a tiring Canadian side, then who knows how it might have played out.

The following weekend we were back in Wales playing Australia in the second pool game. The Australians had begun their World Cup campaign by scoring 91 points against Japan – not a bad start! Gareth Jenkins made some changes after the first game: after their excellent performances off the bench against Canada, Alfie came in at full back, Stephen started at 10 and Colin Charvis came in on the flank. I also got the start again alongside Melon and Bomb. We started slowly and you simply cannot do that against a class side like Australia. Stirling Mortlock kicked a penalty a few minutes into the game, and they went on to score tries through Giteau, Mortlock and Latham in the first half. We suffered early injuries to Alfie and Sonny which meant replacing them and reorganising, but that's no excuse: we were totally dominated. In the second half, we came out determined to repair the damage from the first half, and number 8 Jonathan Thomas barged over for a try. Latham then scored his second and even though we finished with a try from Shane, it didn't hide the fact that we were comfortably beaten. Australia played far better rugby on the day and Berrick Barnes, who started at 10 due to an injury to Stephen Larkham, had a dream first start – we never got near him to put him under any real scrutiny. Final score: Wales 20 Australia 32. The pressure really was on now. We weren't playing well, and many wanted Gareth Jenkins, whose contract was due to expire after the Six Nations 2008, sacked straight away. The Welsh camp was a pretty miserable place to be that night.

We had to get our heads right quite quickly as we only had a five-day turnaround before the third game of the pool against Japan, again in Cardiff. Following on from the defeat to Australia, we knew we had to beat Japan and Fiji in our remaining games – if we did that we could reach the quarter-finals, where we'd likely play South Africa. Gareth Jenkins made a few changes for the game, including TR getting the start at hooker with Huw Bennett on the bench, so I wasn't in the match-day squad, but I was as anxious as those who were playing that we got a win, and a convincing one at that.

The game was a very open affair with both sides trying to get the ball wide and score tries. There were thirteen tries in total, eleven to Wales and two to Japan. Shane and Martyn Williams both scored two apiece. Some of them were excellent – none better than the full-length-of-the-field effort by Japanese right-winger, Kosuke Endo, which was fantastic. The lads got a good run-out, with some getting their first opportunity this World Cup, and having the fans cheering on the boys scoring tries created a very different atmosphere to the previous Saturday. We now had to beat Fiji in the final game of the pool to qualify for the quarter-finals.

After the Japanese win, we didn't play Fiji for more than a week, so were given the weekend off by the coaches. We all went to Longchamp to watch some horse racing and then into Paris for a show. The boys had a great time, and my overriding memory is of being given a police escort down the wrong side of the road on the Champs-Élysées in the coach we travelled on. A great day and night was had by all in the group.

We'd be back in Nantes for the final game against Fiji. The Fijians had beaten Canada, avoided defeat to Japan in a narrow victory and had been hammered by Australia, so were also coming into this game knowing a win would get them into the quarter-finals for the first time since the first World Cup in 1987. During the build-up to the game, the coaches tried to ease the pressure on the players by having as relaxed an atmosphere as possible. If anything, one criticism I'd level at the coaches was that it wasn't as intense as I feel it should have been. Rowland Phillips is a great bloke and likes to have a smile and a joke, but as defence coach, there were times when I felt he needed to have the harder, more disciplined edge that many defensive coaches have. When the side was announced, I was delighted to find I was back in. Alfie captained from full back and in the battle between Hooky and Stephen for the 10 shirt which had gone on throughout the World Cup, a decision was made to accommodate both, with Hooky moving to inside centre and Sonny Parker missing out. The Fijians had many players plying their trade in the top European leagues, such as Vilimoni Delasau, Seru Rabeni, Seremaia Bai, Nicky Little and Akapusi Qera, to name just a few. What occurred over the next few hours will remain with me and many others for years and years to come.

Before the game started, Alfie – who was making his one-hundredth international appearance for Wales, a massive achievement – had *100 caps* specially embroidered into his playing boots and a part of his team talk prior to going out onto the pitch was "Look at my boots, lads – they're lush." Good old Alfie, such a character. If that comment seems to some like we weren't taking the game in hand seriously, then you're completely wrong. We knew Fiji could play: it was just Alfie's way of trying to relieve pressure, and there was plenty of pressure in that camp.

For once in that World Cup, we started really positively. Stephen made a great break and if a few passes had gone to hand, we'd have opened the scoring. We did miss a few opportunities to score tries early on, which came back to haunt us. Fiji were putting in some hits in defence: Rabeni, in particular, was huge and smashed a few of us. Fiji also started to put their attacking game together, and it was Qera who scored the first try of the game after some great handling and running from the Fijians. Shortly after that, the ball went out wide to Delasau and after chipping over Mark Jones, he gathered again from a cruel bounce (from a Welsh perspective!) and was in for another try. Little kicked two penalties before Qera made another break and Leawere went over for their third try, with Little kicking another penalty afterwards. We did score a try with six minutes left in the first half, when Alix Popham picked up at the back of another dominant scrum (one thing that was going well) to score. Qera was sin-binned just before half-time, and we went in 25 points to 10 down. Our defence was all over the place: some players were drifting, some were blitzing up in defence and the Fijians were picking us off at will. The coaches told us in no uncertain terms that we had 40 minutes left to save our World Cup, and with Fiji being down to 14 men for the start of the half, we had to get out there and start quickly.

Almost instantly, Martyn Williams won a turnover, something Nugget was so good at. Shane took the ball in midfield and went on a waltzing dance through their defence, scoring under the posts. I was replaced by TR and just after that (I'm sure just a coincidence), another backs move saw Mark Jones feed Alfie and on his one-hundredth appearance, he scored his fortieth try for his country. The boys were flying at this point, and Peely started another move which ended with Mark Jones scoring in the corner. Stephen kicked the conversion and we were leading 29 points to 25.

Back came Fiji, causing us major problems in defence. Little kicked two penalties to put them back in front. They were really trying to kill the game off but a long pass from Little was picked off by Nugget, who ran in for the score from around 65 metres. With seven minutes to go we were ahead 34 points to 31 – could we finish the game off? Back again came Fiji: Delasau was held up just short of the line, only for prop Graham Dewes to pick up and go over the line amongst a mass of bodies. Had he scored? The matter went to the video referee, who confirmed he had scored. Little kicked the conversion, and Fiji had beaten us 38 points to 34. We were out of the World Cup.

After the game is a bit of a blur. The Fijians were going crazy, and rightly so. I felt numb – I couldn't believe the World Cup had come to an end. To neutrals, it was an unbelievable game to watch, as many have told me. To be honest, I don't care: we lost. Not taking anything away from Fiji, who were brilliant on the day, we made many mistakes, missed out on a number of points due to poor execution and our defence was very poor. Fiji did show ten days later in their quarter-final against South Africa just how good a side they were, leading the Springboks until the last 20 minutes when the South Africans pulled ahead to end up winning 37 points to 20 – and remember South Africa would go on to beat England in the final to become World Champions. But we should have beaten Fiji.

The following day the repercussions started. The players heard that David Pickering and Roger Lewis were going to meet with Gareth Jenkins and the rumour was that he was no longer going to be our coach. Shortly after 10 a.m., Gareth gathered the players together and advised us that this was the case. He thanked us all for our efforts, and also said that he had no regrets – he was very emotional. The media had got wind of the news so there were a number of journalists in and around the hotel. We all got on the coach and travelled to the airport to catch the flight home in a very subdued atmosphere.

Once we landed, the plan was to go back to the Vale of Glamorgan hotel for debriefing, but Gareth knew that there would be a huge media circus there, so he made the decision to get off the coach early to avoid this. The overriding memory I have of the World Cup is Gareth Jenkins forlornly walking away from his players with just a carrier bag in his hand, no longer coach of Wales.

Looking back over his time as coach, I'd say I didn't feel the coaching team was strong enough: there needed to be someone in there with a real steely edge. There was also not enough experience from an international perspective. I have a lot of respect for Gareth Jenkins: he gave me my chance at the Scarlets and before he came in as Welsh coach, my international career was very stop-start. The man had dreamt for many years of being the Wales coach and he'd fulfilled that dream. He's a passionate Welshman and rugby man and was crushed when his time in international rugby didn't work out as hoped. He trusted the players to play what they saw in front of them and the players loved him for some of his quirks, such as when he announced the team to the players but forgot who was playing in certain positions and had to turn to Nigel Davies to help him. He's a great rugby man and that final vision of him walking away from us all after the 2007 World Cup isn't a nice image of the end of his coaching period to have in your memory. But at the end of that disappointing tournament I was going home to my new young family, wondering – as I'm sure were others – who the next Wales coach was going to be.

CHAPTER 7

Seasons of Many Changes

AFTER A GREAT European campaign, the Scarlets came into a new season in 2007–08 full of hope and confidence. As we were in a World Cup year and a number of our first team players were away with Wales and also our captain, Simon Easterby, with Ireland, we were missing a number of our stars at the beginning. I think we were all a bit concerned that the start of the season would be a struggle.

As it turned out, the season started reasonably well. By the end of October, we were sitting in second place in the Celtic League with victories against Ospreys, Connacht, Leinster and Ulster. But in November, even though we now had the international players back in the fold after the World Cup, we suffered some disappointing results, including a League defeat to Edinburgh and two defeats in the Heineken Cup to Clermont Auvergne and London Wasps. In December we lost home and away in the Heineken Cup to Munster. Fans and players alike were hugely disappointed with how the season was progressing – particularly off the back off the previous spring, when we'd been serious contenders, especially in Europe.

Phil Davies and us players were under pressure. Phil's an honest hard-working man and a good coach. He's very good at planning sessions and gave the players six-week schedule plans detailing training requirements, games you were down to play in, etc. – as a player I really liked having that level of detail.

What I would say is that when the pressure was on, his team meetings and our analysis of games (which he always played a huge part in) became a bit excessive, as did the training sessions. The most successful sessions were short and sharp with high levels of intensity and players felt they were getting real value out of them.

Into 2008 the results were getting worse – especially in Europe, where we suffered a heavy away loss to London Wasps by 40 points to 7. Less than a week later, it got worse still, with a home defeat to Clermont Auvergne by 41 points to nil. On the night in the pouring rain at Stradey Park, we were punished by a far superior side. We were bullied up front with players such as Mario Ledesma, Martin Scelzo, Julien Bonnaire and Elvis Vermeulen having a field day. They scored six tries on the night and we were totally dominated, a humbling experience. We ended our European campaign for the season on that defeat, without one single point in the campaign. It was a massive disappointment for all of us.

Just days before the Clermont defeat, news broke that did nothing to improve the mood around the place. It was announced that Dwayne Peel would be leaving Llanelli Scarlets to join Sale Sharks at the end of the season. This was a huge blow to both the players and the fans. Peely was Llanelli Scarlets through and through. A local lad who loved the place, for him to be leaving spoke volumes of how he saw the region going. Peely loved playing at a high tempo, with his pace plus his passing ability and his quick-tap penalties to catch defenders whose concentration levels had dropped, but he'd seen things changing within the region and with an increased salary being offered at Sale, decided his future was elsewhere. It was a big setback to lose such an outstanding player for the Scarlets, and also playing in England put his international chances for Wales in jeopardy. Peely and Mike Phillips were really pushing each other close for the starting Welsh scrum half position and now with Mike being the only one of the two playing in Wales, in all likelihood he was going to get the edge. I respected Peely's decision, but the players and I were massively disappointed, considering what we'd achieved the previous season, to lose such a class player who'd done so much for the region.

We might have been out of the cup competitions, but in the League we were still doing well in March, sitting in second place. However, after three consecutive defeats in April we slipped to fifth place. The board, fans and players were unhappy and come the end of April, a decision was taken to make a change on the coaching front. Phil Davies was relieved of his duties: he was leaving.

It was sad to see Phil go. As said earlier, I have plenty of time for him as a man and as also as a rugby coach. Only one year earlier, he'd led us to the semi-finals of the Heineken Cup and now he was moving on. What many may not know is that Phil played a massive part in the planning of the new stadium at Parc y Scarlets. As mentioned earlier, he was a man of great detail, and in terms of the layout of the training facilities, the changing rooms, the hospitality boxes, etc., he had a lot of input into the plan. Now, unfortunately, he wasn't going to be part of the region when we moved there – a real shame.

Prior to Phil's departure, there were strong rumours that New Zealand internationals Greg Somerville and number 8 Mose Tuiali'i, who were both playing with the Canterbury Crusaders, could be joining the region. There were also links to Australian back-row players David Lyons and Rocky Elsom. These were proven international players and you did wonder – if we had made these kind of moves around the start of the season, we'd have been so much stronger and who knows, perhaps Phil and Peely could have remained. But we were where we were. A signing that certainly had been made was Simon Maling. A lock forward who'd played for New Zealand and also out in Japan, would be joining for the new season.

After Phil's departure, Paul Moriarty was put in temporary charge and was assisted by Robert Jones. Both were already at the region as forwards and backs coaches respectively, so knew the players and had respect from us all. The pair remained in charge up to the end of a very disappointing season and they, like us, pretty much knew that come the start of the new season there'd be new people in charge of the region and the move to our new home at Parc Y Scarlets.

In May it was announced that we would indeed have a new Head Coach: Nigel Davies. Nige, like Gareth Jenkins and Phil, knew the region, the fans and environment very well. Nigel Davies hadn't only been a player for Llanelli for many years but had also been an assistant coach to Gareth Jenkins at the club and region. In the same month, David Lyons was announced as a new signing to the region. Lyons was joining to replace the departing Alix Popham, who was going to Brive. I loved playing with Pops so was sad to see him go, but as time proved, Lyons was a fine player for the region. May also saw Matthew J Watkins and Ben Broster leaving us, and incoming we did have a New Zealander coming in as prop – though not Greg Somerville, but Kees Meeuws joining from Castres. Meeuws was an outstanding New Zealand international and had had a good stint out in France. I was really pleased with that signing and was very much looking forward to playing alongside him in the front row.

In the summer it was announced that assisting Nige in coaching duties would be Paul Moriarty, staying on as forwards coach, and coming in was John Muggleton, who'd been Australian defence coach when they won the World Cup in 1999. Another new face to the region was another Aussie, Brad Harrington, as fitness coach. These incoming coaches meant that leaving the region were Robert Jones and Wayne Proctor. They're two guys I have loads of respect for, and they did a great job for the Llanelli Scarlets.

The new season was going to be really interesting with all the changes behind the scenes. The decision was made to change the regional name to just 'the Scarlets', plus we'd be moving into a new stadium before Christmas. There was the question of how the squad would gel with the changes in personnel, with players such as Peely, Pops and Matthew J no longer there. In the hooker position, I had a real battle on my hands to be a regular in the side, as we also had Ken Owens, Emyr Phillips and Samoan international Mahonri Schwalger, a signing made by Phil Davies, on our books.

We started the League season really well, playing particularly well against Connacht and scoring some great tries – seven in total. Jonathan Davies came on as a second-half replacement in that game, showing us all what ability he had on a rugby field. Foxy was only 20 at the time and not a regular in the side at that point, but it was only going to be a matter of time. You could see just from training with the young centre what a rugby talent he was and that he had a long successful career ahead of him, injuries allowing.

In the Heineken Cup, we started off at home to the English side, Harlequins. We started really well, scoring some great tries, though also missing a few gilt-edged opportunities. Harlequins made the most of our errors and came out on top, 29 points to 22 winners. The following weekend we were in Paris to play Stade Français. The Paris-based side were far too good for us. They went through the gears in the second half in particular, winning by 37 points to 15. We'd now lost 9 consecutive matches in the Heineken Cup: simply not good enough for a team who had been semi-finalists only two seasons earlier. For fans, European success must have seemed a long time ago. We were working hard to turn things around, but some new players just weren't of the same quality as players who'd left, and some of those still there from two years earlier were no longer playing at the same standard.

28th November 2008 was the date of our first ever home game at the Parc Y Scarlets – the Scarlets' new home and a stadium with fantastic facilities. We were all sad to leave Stradey Park, a place that had seen so many memorable matches and which will always hold a place in the hearts of all those who played or cheered their team on there, but now we had a new place to play and make memories. The first game was against Munster in the League. I wasn't selected – Ken got the start at hooker with Schwalger on the bench. There was a good crowd, but the game unfortunately resulted in a loss for us by 16 points to 10 – another close game we could have won – and frustration amongst the players and the coaches was growing.

Back into Europe, we lost away to Ulster before drawing against them at home the following week, which at least meant that our losing streak in Europe had finally had come to an end. Next up was the return game against Stade Français and on the day we really clicked, showing just what we could do when we got it right. We scored three tries in total, one through David Lyons and the other two coming from Foxy, who got the start in the centre alongside Regan. We won by 31 points to 17 and the coaches and players were very satisfied with our efforts that day. But could we back it up?

The following week we lost at home to Harlequins by 29 points to 24. I scored a rare try but it was no consolation: another European campaign was over at the group stages without being even close to qualification. That season I was in the last year of my contract and was considering my playing options. It was going reasonably well with Wales, but there's no doubt the loss of Peely and no real progression in Europe did make me wonder if my future lay elsewhere after five seasons at the Scarlets.

As my contract was running down, I did get some interest from French side Clermont Auvergne, who were turning into a real powerhouse in France and in Europe. There were some initial discussions, but when I thought about my family, with Brooke being really young, and also how much I loved playing for and living in Wales, it did make me doubt whether this was the right move for me. I spoke to Warren Gatland at the time and he very much wanted me to stay in Wales and further my international career, saying that they'd keep a closer eye on my performances and how I was progressing as a player, so that made my mind up.

After the British and Irish Lions tour, I re-signed for the Scarlets. Not so many Welsh players seem to be moving abroad recently, but I totally understand the reasons why some do. The decision has to be made by the individual involved and does depend on where they're at with their career. Are they at the end of their international career with players coming through in their position, and so a chance of few years playing out of Wales and making some serious money might be good? Players' careers can be short so it's a massive decision to make.

The summer of 2009 saw the release of Simon Maling, who'd struggled to make a real impact due to injuries. Amongst others, Gavin and Nathan Thomas also left, as did Kees Meeuws. Kees was a player I loved playing alongside: a great guy who was immensely strong – a human colossus. Dafydd James was also on the move. Daf was a fantastic player for the Scarlets, scoring many important tries especially in Europe, and another I was sorry to see go. Paul Moriarty also made the decision to leave as forwards coach, opening up an opportunity for Simon Easterby to help out with the forwards whilst remaining in a playing role within the squad. With Easters moving into coaching, the captaincy role fell vacant and Mark Jones, a player who'd bounced back from numerous injuries and always gave his all for the region, was appointed.

We had a number of players coming in, including prop Rhys Thomas, Scottish winger Sean Lamont, centre Gareth Maule and two young players from the Welsh Premiership in Tavis Knoyle and Ben Morgan (from Neath and Merthyr respectively), who both became very good regional players and went on to play for their countries. I still went into the season fearing that perhaps we were a bit short on quality and worrying about the strength of the squad, but I hoped I'd be proved wrong.

In the League, we won the opening game at home to Leinster but then lost the next four games – not the greatest way to go into the start of your campaign. First game up in the Heineken Cup was at home to Brive. We had a few players missing from the line-up and had to play Sean Lamont in the centre alongside Foxy. Appearing for Brive that day was my mate Alix Popham and I knew given half the chance, he'd look to smash a few of us, as you'd expect. On the day we played reasonably well and we got the win by 24 points to 12. It made a pleasant change to be starting a European competition with a victory. Unfortunately, we then lost the next three games in Europe, away to London Irish and back-to-back losses to Leinster, home and away. Leinster won the group and we had to be content to move into the second-tier competition, the Amlin Challenge Cup, where we played Toulon. The French team had huge financial backing and in their line-up for that match were players such as Sonny Bill Williams, Jonny Wilkinson and Matt Henjak. They had far too much for us on the day and ran out convincing winners by 38 points to 12. Toulon got to the final that year but were beaten in Marseille by Cardiff Blues, in a huge upset. Seeing Cardiff Blues dismiss them like they did after Toulon had soundly beaten us showed the work required for the Scarlets to be a threat again in Europe.

In the League, I didn't play in as many games as I'd have liked due to a few injuries, plus international duties. During the season, defence coach John Muggleton had announced he was leaving the region at the end of the season. There's no doubting Muggleton's credentials as a coach, but I and others found him very arrogant and not someone you got on with personally, so I wasn't going to miss him.

Just before the start of the 2010–11 season, Simon Easterby was unfortunately forced to retire due to injury. Easters was a fantastic player and his presence on the rugby field was going to be missed. With his retirement, Easters was able to concentrate on his coaching duties full time. The big news for me personally in the run-up to the start of the season was that I was asked to become captain of the Scarlets by Nigel Davies. I was chuffed to bits to be offered the role – it was a huge honour, and frankly a bit daunting. However, with senior players such as Iestyn Thomas, David Lyons, Vernon Cooper and Stephen Jones there giving me great support and advice when needed on the field, I was in safe hands.

The forthcoming season was leading up to the next World Cup in New Zealand, so it was important for me to be in good form to ensure selection for Wales. In our first game in the Magners League, we lost away to a new side in the tournament, Benetton Treviso. We'd rested a few players for the game (including myself), and the Italians made the most of it, running out 34 points to 28 victors. The match marked the Scarlets debut of a certain 18-year-old winger called George North, who ran in two tries on the night, but it was a very disappointing loss.

Our first outing in Europe that season was at home to Perpignan. In a fantastic game of rugby where both sides combined scored nine tries, we came out on top with a scoreline of 43 points to 34. Stephen Jones scored 28 points in total and was fantastic, as was Josh Turnbull, who played openside flanker and was everywhere, causing problems for the opposition on the day. The following weekend we took on the Leicester Tigers at Welford Road and they took us apart. Leicester were the English League Champions at the time – they were outstanding and we just couldn't live with them, especially in the second half.

Prior to Christmas we played Benetton Treviso in Europe in back-to-back games and gained two victories, so going into the New Year we were still in contention in Europe this time. In the League we were doing reasonably well, sitting in second place, but then we got hammered by the Ospreys just after Christmas when they put 60 points on us in a night to forget at the Liberty Stadium. We were totally dominated in all areas of the game, and my opposite number being Richard Hibbard – my main rival for the starting hooker slot for Wales – made it far worse for me. A horrible night for us against a star-studded Ospreys team.

At the beginning of 2011, we lost another Scarlets stalwart when Dafydd Jones was forced to retire due to injury, having not played for more than a year due to damage to his shoulder. He was a fabulous back-row player and with him and Easters out, the replacement players had some big shoes to fill. In January we faced Leicester Tigers at home, determined to get revenge for the heavy defeat inflicted on us at Welford Road. There was a fantastic atmosphere at Parc Y Scarlets and we started well, leading at half-time. However, similarly to the first game, their power up front aided them in moving away from us, and they ran out winners by 32 points to 18. The loss left us with one game left away to Perpignan, still in with a chance of qualification from the pool. We knew it would be tough but we still hoped we could progress.

Perpignan exerted all their renowned forward power on us, with one of the best front rows in Europe in Perry Freshwater, Marius Tincu and Nicolas Mas. Due to injuries, we had a young tight head starting – Simon Gardiner – who under the circumstances did very well with myself and Iestyn alongside him. Perpignan ran out easy winners by 37 points to 5, scoring five tries in the process. It had been an improved performance in Europe, but ultimately we came up short again. In the League, we ended the season in fifth place, missing out on the play-offs. We had some really exciting players but were struggling against the best teams with forward power, something we had to rectify if we wanted to be serious competitors.

The season ended on a sour note for me after news broke that David Lyons, an outstanding player for us, was going to Stade Français in the summer. A deal had been struck and a decision was made that for the last few games of the season, Lyons wouldn't be risked just in case he picked up an injury and potentially ruined this big-money move. This didn't sit well with me at all: you want to play your best players and I wasn't happy to have a player as good as him, fit, and sitting games out. Lyons was a great number 8, perhaps not the greatest trainer, but he more than made up for that on game day. Luckily, Ben Morgan was emerging as a player of real promise at 8, so he would be the man to take over the position.

We also already knew that next season we would be without another of our stars: Regan King was off to Clermont Auvergne.

We had good young players in the region such as Liam Williams, George North, Jonathan Davies, Ken Owens, Josh Turnbull and Rob McCusker, but when you're losing established stars due to retirement or them deciding to try their luck elsewhere and those coming in are not yet up to that standard, it's very difficult to progress as a region.

At the start of the 2011–12 season, we were missing myself through injury and Ken Owens on international duty, as well as other players still recovering after the World Cup, so our squad strength was really going to be tested. I returned from my neck operation in October, when I was on the bench for the Ulster game. I did start our first European game that season, against Castres at home, a match we won by 31 points to 23. The following weekend we travelled to Northampton to face a team who had forwards of the calibre of Soane Tonga'uiha, Dylan Hartley, Brian Mujati, Courtney Lawes and Tom Wood, just to name a few, so we knew we were in for a real battle up front. We played really well and got the victory. It was a massive boost to our confidence to come to Franklin's Gardens and gain an away victory. Unfortunately, we lost the next three pool games in Europe so again, we didn't gain qualification to the latter stages. Though we did beat Castres in the last pool game, it was a case of too little, too late.

In the RaboDirect Pro 12 League (as it was now known), we finished out of the play-offs. In April we also lost to retirement another player who had been a stalwart of the region: Iestyn Thomas had to retire due to a neck injury. He'd given so much to the jersey – he's one of the best scrummaging loose-head props I've ever played with, and he deserved to have won more international caps. He was definitely missed both on and off the field.

In June 2012, it was announced that coach Nigel Davies was leaving us to join Gloucester as Director of Rugby, having decided he needed a new rugby challenge. Gloucester had some financial backing and were looking to progress. To replace him, Scarlets made the decision to promote from within. Simon

Easterby was to become the head coach, with Mark Jones becoming the attack coach – two men who only a few years earlier I had been taking the rugby field with as teammates. Brad Harrington stayed on as strength and conditioning coach and we had a new face in Danny Wilson, coming in as forwards coach. I'd worked with Danny for Wales when he occasionally used to come in for a few days in training squads to work on line-out techniques, and I liked how he coached and communicated with the players. From the brief time I'd spent with him, I felt he was a bright young coach with a good future in the game.

With a new coaching group on board, a change was also made at captain, with Rob McCusker being named. Rob was a big character and a fine player in the back row, and it made sense for a new voice to come in. I had no issues with the captaincy being passed on – for me, I felt it was a good decision at the right time. Rob had been with the region for six seasons, he knew the environment, and it allowed me to concentrate on my own game. Having Easters and Mark coaching us was odd initially. Easters had gone very quickly from being one of the boys to now being the Head Coach. His working hours changed, and he now had to deal with structures and selections, etc. Having said that, the transition was pretty smooth, bearing all this in mind. Easters was a coach who was intense in training and if things weren't going as well as he'd have liked, he himself got involved in sessions, with different drills to show by example what he wanted.

In the League yet again we started well, even being top come October, but a few heavy defeats including another to our West Wales rivals, Ospreys, meant that at the end of the League season we finished in fourth place. Finishing fourth did mean we qualified for the play-offs, but we were heavily beaten by Ulster at Ravenhill at the semi-final stage – a disappointment for the players and fans not to have a day out at a final.

The European campaign was, to be honest, very disappointing. We lost every game, including two thrashings by

Clermont Auvergne, home and away. We picked up two points from the whole campaign, for losing bonus points. It was a dire tournament for us. During the season it was announced that Ben Morgan and Stephen Jones – two key players – would be leaving. Stephen's a legend at the Scarlets and rightly so – a fantastic rugby player. Morgan Stoddart was also retiring. I'd also made a big rugby decision: I was going to leave the Scarlets. After nine seasons, I needed a fresh challenge.

My decision to leave came down to a few things. Firstly, I wasn't getting as much game time as I wanted. Secondly, being 32 at the time, I felt my career would be coming to an end soon (how wrong I was!), and I wanted a new challenge before I hung up my boots. In the Autumn of 2012 I told Easters of my feelings, which he totally understood, and in January 2013, I signed a two year deal with Cardiff Blues starting the following season. The coach at Cardiff Blues at the time was Phil Davies, who I obviously knew from his time at the Scarlets. He spoke to me about how he saw me fitting in and helping some of the younger players coming through. I also knew quite a few of the boys playing for Cardiff Blues, who advised me about the environment there. I was very impressed with what I heard. Travelling from my home in Tonyrefail to Cardiff rather than to West Wales was another factor to weigh up in my final decision. The Scarlets did offer me a new deal but my mind was made up: I was going to play for Cardiff Blues.

I look back at my time with the Scarlets very fondly, and my only real regret is that at the end of the 2012–13 season I didn't play as much as I'd have liked, to say goodbye to the fans. Obviously thinking about the following seasons ahead, Easters kept picking Ken and Kirby Myhill or Emyr Phillips, but I'd have loved to play a few of those games at the end of the season and I felt my form warranted selection.

Even now when I go back to the Scarlets, the fans and the employees treat me fantastically well. I loved my time there. I played with some fantastic players and made some great friends for life – including Iestyn Thomas, my car buddy for all those years of travelling back and forth. It was an honour to play there for nine seasons and especially to be captain for two of them, the standout season being 2006–07. I'll always be grateful to them for taking me from the defunct Celtic Warriors and turning me into an international player. A great place with knowledgeable fans – just a fantastic place to play rugby and one I'll always have fond memories of.

CHAPTER 8

A New Era - Gats & Co.

ON 9TH NOVEMBER 2007 it was announced that Warren Gatland would become the Head Coach of Wales. Gats, as he's known in all walks of life, was known to all Welsh rugby players through his very impressive rugby CV, plus the fact that most of us had at some time in our careers played against a team coached by him. When he was given the role, already on his rugby résumé were three Premiership titles, a European Challenge Cup and the Heineken Cup, all with London Wasps, plus an Air New Zealand Cup victory with Waikato, from whom Wales had secured his services. Gats had also previously coached internationally with Ireland for three years, so knew the Six Nations and European rugby as a whole. For us players, getting a coach of the calibre of this man was exciting and we were really looking forward to working with him.

Prior to Gats officially taking charge on 1st December 2007, Wales had a game against South Africa coming up, which Nigel Davies was asked to take charge of. South Africa had become World Champions only a few months earlier so it was going to be a huge challenge. When the team was announced, playing at hooker would be Huw Bennett with TR Thomas on the bench. Getting his first cap that day was Morgan Stoddart, who'd been in outstanding form for Llanelli Scarlets and fully deserved his opportunity. Melon was given the huge honour of being named captain. As a friend of mine and someone I'd played alongside through the different age groups, then at Ponty and then into regional rugby, I was chuffed to bits for him and felt it was fully deserved.

We played quite well on the day, Stoddart scoring a try on his debut and also being heavily involved in the first Welsh try, scored by Colin Charvis, but South Africa were a fine side and ran in five tries of their own through Juan Smith, Jaque Fourie (with two), JP Pietersen and Ryan Kankowski. The final scoreline was Wales 12 South Africa 34. The year 2007, a turbulent one for Wales from an international rugby perspective, had come to an end. What would 2008, under the tutelage of Warren Gatland, bring?

Gats initially had to get a coaching staff in place, and he made the decision to keep Neil Jenkins and Robin McBryde, from the previous regime under Gareth Jenkins, on as coaches. Also joining the coaching staff would be Rob Howley. Howlers had been a Welsh international and had captained his country numerous times, so fully understood Welsh rugby and the pressure that came with it, plus had played under Gats to huge success with London Wasps. Finishing off the coaching group was Shaun Edwards. Shaun had worked alongside Gats with London Wasps, becoming Head Coach when Gats left and guiding them to another Heineken Cup. Shaun was highly thought of in England and many wanted him involved in the English international side. He'd been offered the England Saxons role – in old rugby terms, the England B coaching position. With Shaun deciding instead to come to Wales to work as assistant to Gats, it was a major coup for us.

Gats' first ever squad was announced for our first game of the Six Nations 2008, which was a huge test at Twickenham against England. The English had got to the World Cup Final the previous year, and their confidence must have been high. Gats sprang a surprise in the first squad announcement: he'd convinced Martyn Williams to come out of retirement. Nugget had decided to retire from international rugby after the World Cup, but the plans Gats had for Wales had convinced him to come back. Gats had also made the decision that we'd have a new captain in place, and that man would be Ryan Jones. The selection of Ryan was a bit of a surprise to many, what with senior players such as Stephen Jones, Dwayne Peel and Melon all in the squad, but Gats had seen in Ryan a man who had a real presence, and he was also in very good form with his side, the Ospreys, who were also playing really well at the time. Gavin Henson was also named in the squad and there was only one uncapped player – a young full back/winger at the time called Jamie Roberts, who over the years turned out to be a mainstay in the centre. I also received a call-up, along with Huw Bennett as my challenger for the number 2 shirt.

In the early squad sessions, you could sense a change in mentality and the intensity had been turned up a few notches in terms of how we were going to be coached. The structure that Gats had had in place with the London Wasps was for forwards to do the basics such as scrum and line-out well, but also to work hard when in possession of the ball. He wanted us to carry around the corner of rucks and mauls and then when the time was right to release the backs, who by then hopefully would have mismatches with the opposition forwards up against them. We had some X-factor players in our backs, such as Shane and Byrney, and with Stephen Jones controlling things at 10, we had the nucleus of a decent side with the right game plan in place and the correct execution by the players.

Gats also made it clear from the very beginning that your family comes first. He told us all that if we had any family issues, we should let him and the coaches know and they'd do all they could to help. Also in each camp I've ever been in with him, at the initial team meeting when you first meet up, he congratulates and welcomes any new faces to the squad and also gives praise to any players from regions that are going really well in their respective competitions. It brings a really nice feel to the group and really helps with squad bonding.

The rugby sessions were short and intense, with periods of rest. Training sessions with Gats and the coaches was another level to what we'd done previously. The sessions were shorter but you were flat out, being constantly put under pressure to make swift decisions. All of us were having questions asked of our ability. The intensity was almost at Test match level, which now looking back with hindsight, was what we'd lacked previously in training in my time with the Wales set-up.

Defence was a very important feature we concentrated on. Shaun put a totally different structure in place: line speed is huge to Shaun, as is communication to your team-mates when in a defensive line, so players around you know where you are, which helps keep that line in place. Shaun's ethos, then as now, is 'get off the line and smoke someone'. He wants players to be aggressive in defence and use it as an attacking weapon. He's a coach with a real edge – someone you always want to try your best for, and one of the best I've ever worked with.

When Gats announced his first ever starting side, he selected 13 Ospreys, including Huw at hooker. The two others were Nugget, starting at 7, and Mark Jones starting on the wing. I had to make do with a place on the bench. The Ospreys were going really well at the time so the number selected wasn't that big a surprise to the players, but Gats did take a bit of stick from the press. We hadn't won at Twickenham in 20 years and very few, if any, thought that was about to change.

Straight from the kick-off we conceded a penalty that Jonny Wilkinson kicked over. Hooky kicked a penalty to level the scores, only for Wilkinson to kick one of his trademark drop goals. England then scored a try when debutant Lesley Vainikolo got the beating of Mark Jones in an aerial cross-field kick and then offloaded to Toby Flood to score. At half-time England were 16 points to 6 up and Gats and Shaun were pointing out the turnovers we were conceding, telling us to keep hold of the ball and we'd get opportunities. At the start of the second half, Wilkinson kicked another penalty, but after that, we started to gain some territory and play some good rugby. In defence, we were knocking them back and putting them under pressure. I was brought on after 58 minutes to replace Huw. The pressure we were putting on England really began to pay, with Wilkinson making a rare error – after a great break, Hooky offloaded to Lee Byrne, who scored a brilliant try. Hooky kicked the conversion. Shortly afterwards, Mike Phillips charged down a clearance kick by Ian Balshaw, Melon picked up the ball and passed it on to Nugget, who got it on to AWJ, who gave it to Mike Phillips, who reached out over the try line to dot the ball down for a try. Hooky kicked the conversion off the touchline and we were in front!

The last ten minutes was really pleasing. We controlled the ball and showed great man-management and in truth, England didn't look like scoring. The referee, Craig Joubert, blew the whistle and we'd finally won at Twickenham after 20 years. The players and coaches celebrated on the pitch after this great victory. After only two months of Gats being in charge, we'd beaten England, a team who only a few months earlier had been in a World Cup Final and who had also, just prior to the World Cup, put 60 points on us. After the win, Shaun brought in a song that was then played regularly whenever we had a victory to bring the boys together, 'Saturday Night at the Movies' by The Drifters.

The following week we were at home against Scotland. There were a few changes to the starting fifteen, Jamie Roberts getting his first start on the right wing and Tom Shanklin coming into the centre. Huw again got the start at hooker and I was named on the bench. The game was a close affair: Shane Williams and Hooky scored tries but Chris Paterson kicked five penalties, keeping them in the game. With 20 minutes to go, I came on and Gats also decided to change the half-backs, bringing on Dwayne Peel and Stephen Jones for Mike Phillips and Hooky. We gained a bit more control and moved away when Shane scored another try; Stephen Jones kicked the conversion and also kicked two penalties. We ran out 30 points to 15 winners. Two wins from two.

For the third game of the tournament, against Italy, Gats made a few changes. I got the start at hooker, Melon also started and so did Rhys Thomas, so we had a whole new front row compared to the previous games. Following on from the Scotland game and their impressive performances, Peely and Stephen also got starts at 9 and 10 respectively. We led early on through two penalties from Stephen Jones, but the first try was scored by the Italians. We had a line-out close to our line and my throw was long, the ball going straight into the waiting arms of Martín Castrogiovanni, who went over for the try. I was totally gutted but had to shake that error off and concentrate on my game. At half-time, we were only 13 points to 8 up. Gats told us in the interval that our fitness would kick in after 50–60 mins and we'd blow them away, which as it turned out was true. In the second half we really put in a strong performance, with Lee Byrne getting two tries, Tom Shanklin scoring a try on his fiftieth appearance and Shane Williams getting two more. Stephen Jones scored 20 points on the day as well. The final score was Wales 47 Italy 8. We'd got three wins from three and next up would be Ireland for the Triple Crown.

In terms of the Italy game, I was pleased with my performance bar the one line-out error which had resulted in a try, and I was really hoping I'd done enough to get the nod for the Irish game. Gats was getting some stick in the Irish media, which was to be expected as a former coach of their national team. When Gats announced the side I was disappointed to find I'd be back on the bench, as Huw got the nod at hooker. But as events were to unfold, I would indeed get to start.

On the morning of the match, Huw went down with a sickness bug. I was told a few hours before kick-off that I'd be starting and, as my back-up, Gareth Williams of the Cardiff Blues was flown over to sit on the bench. I was very nervous prior to the game – I was going to start a match in which Wales could potentially win the Triple Crown! But it was a great opportunity and I wanted to make the most of it.

The Irish started the game by keeping the ball in the forwards and playing very tight. When they did release the ball to the backs then it went as far as Ronan O'Gara, who kept us pinned back with his accurate kicking. The game was tight throughout and some great defence in the first half from Mike Phillips stopped Shane Horgan just short of the try line. Just prior to half-time, Mike was yellow carded for foul play and we knew that for the next ten minutes we had our work cut out for us. However, despite being down to 14 men, we managed to score a try through a bit of brilliance from Shane Williams (yet again!), who got past Andrew Trimble to touch down in the corner. It was Shane's fortieth try for Wales, equalling Alfie's record – and what a game to do it in. Stephen Jones kicked a great conversion to put us 7 points up. Mike returned to the field with Ireland putting us under real pressure. Nugget was next to get a yellow card, due to a trip on Eoin Reddan. O'Gara kicked the resulting penalty and then added another, meaning it was now a one-point game. We were gamely hanging on when we secured a penalty that Stephen kicked over – we'd won the Triple Crown, the first win in Ireland for eight years, and now we were moving on to play France in Cardiff for the Grand Slam. On a personal note, in the line-out we had 100% success on our ball, and when you have Paul O'Connell in the opposition line-up, that's some achievement.

In the build-up to the Grand Slam game against the French, training was obviously intense. Every player in the squad was desperate to start and in a few positions, the decision on who'd get the start was really close. One such position was at hooker. Huw had now overcome his bug prior to the Irish game and was fully fit. He'd started against England and Scotland and I'd got the start against Italy and Ireland. A few days before the game Gats took me to one side and told me the decision of who to start at hooker had been a really close call, but that the line-out that went awry against Italy had gone against me and they'd decided to go with Huw. I was absolutely gutted, but I appreciated how honest Gats had been with me, and that he'd given me a reason for the decision.

The game itself was very tight in the first half with Hooky kicking three penalties to Jean-Baptiste Élissalde's two. In the

Back in the day, in Tonyrefail Primary football team (top row, third from left).

Look at that smile... Maybe this is where my nickname came from?

One of my first articles in the local paper for my rugby achievements, along with Cookie.

RHONDDA Schools under-16 players Geraint Cooke and Matthew Rees have produced remarkable displays this season.

Full-back Cooke and Rees, who is a hooker, both attend Tonyrefail Comprehensive School.

Cooke won a place in the Wales under-16 side which played Portugal and Rees, despite showing brilliant form, failed to catch the selectors' eyes.

"Both these players have a big future in the game," said Rhondda Schools coach Chris Jones.

Jones said Llanelli coach Gareth Jenkins was very impressed with the two players when he saw them in action at the Oval.

On my teenage window-cleaning round!

Receiving Player of the Year for Tonyrefail U15s, presented by Nigel Benzani.

Tonyrefail Youth friendly against a French touring team (top row, third from left).

Early days: playing for Treorchy against Llanharan in 2000 – guess the second row.

The beginning of my professional career – playing for Pontypridd.

(© Huw Evans)

Celtic Warriors squad in its one season in existence, 2003–04. From the results we achieved and looking at the players we had, it had so much potential (top row, third from right).

(© Huw Evans)

Scarlets' Heineken Cup quarter final against Munster, 2007 – making yet another break in the wide channel.
(© Huw Evans)

Not often would I cross the whitewash, but I enjoyed this try for the Scarlets in the 2007 Heineken Cup semi final against Leicester. It was a shame we didn't make the final.
(© Huw Evans)

The ice baths – I won't miss these after I finish playing. Sonny Parker laughs as Melon tries to tense his abs!
(© Huw Evans)

2008: my first Grand Slam! I enjoyed the battle with Huw Bennett for the number 2 jersey.

(© Huw Evans)

Taking on Sergio Parisse, one of the most talented players in world rugby, with the Scarlets.

(© Huw Evans)

Leaving the Vale for Pennyhill Park at the start of the Lions journey, 2009. L–R: Andy Powell, Alun Wyn Jones, Shane Williams, Tommy Bowe, me, Jamie Roberts, Bomb, Melon, Nugget, Stephen Jones and Mike Phillips

(© Huw Evans)

Bomb, myself and Melon in the week leading up to the second Lions Test, 2009. The first all-Welsh Lions front row since 1955.

(© Getty Images)

The picture says it all. With Jamie Heaslip, feeling dejected after the final whistle in the Lions' second Test against the Boks.

(© Getty Images)

Don't mess with the French forwards. This was caused by me stopping a Brive second row being able to lift at the line-out – the next ruck, this happened!

(© Huw Evans)

I'm sure he said there were some seals around here… A trip to Wellington with Wales (with Stephen Jones, Ken Owens and Foxy).
(© Huw Evans)

Admiring the view on a helicopter trip around Wellington.
(© Huw Evans)

Duties of a captain leading up to a Test match: facing the media alongside Gats.
(© Huw Evans)

Up against one of my toughest opponents, Richie McCaw – I'm sure I'm speaking on behalf a lot of rugby players.

(© Huw Evans)

Things you do for the team as captain: taking a telling off from Alain Rolland.

(© Huw Evans)

2012: what a feeling! My second Grand Slam and my 50th cap to go with it!

(© Huw Evans)

My first game for Cardiff Blues: Worcester away in a friendly, 2013.

(© Huw Evans)

Sam Warburton, Harry Robinson, Ellis Jenkins and Cory Allen shave their heads as part of Cardiff Blues' fundraising for Velindre.

(© Huw Evans)

Wales trials, 2014: Probables vs Possibles, a one-off game. Probables were way too strong for us that day – the look on my face says it all.
(© Huw Evans)

One of my last caps for Wales in the summer of 2014, after beating cancer.
(© Huw Evans)

Taking on London Irish for Cardiff Blues, 2014.
(© Huw Evans)

Playing my part at a Cardiff Blues Christmas party for the supporters' kids.

(© Huw Evans)

Against Leinster with Cardiff Blues, 2016.

(© Huw Evans)

v Benetton Treviso in 2016.

(© Huw Evans)

Lining up my opposite number, Leonardo Ghiraldini, in a European Challenge Cup match v Toulouse, 2018. A memorable cup campaign for Cardiff Blues.

(© Huw Evans)

Family photo. From L–R: Julian, Lisa, me, my mother and Martin.

Me and my mother.

The day I shaved my head, with the support of my Uncle Dave and my mate Scott.

Day at the races with my dad
and his partner Maggie.

I'm so proud of my
wonderful daughter, Brooke.

Happy families: with Becky
and Brooke.

With Andrew and Kylie, who are in charge of fundraising for Velindre.

The amazing staff nurses who treated me. I can't thank the staff at Velindre enough for everything they did for me – I owe them my life.

second half, play started opening up a bit. Henson was yellow carded and whilst he was off the pitch, France levelled the scores. Just before the hour mark I was brought on, as was Stephen Jones. A few minutes later, David Skrela threw out a pass to Yannick Jauzion, who made a bit of a mess of it. Shane was on it like a flash, showing great speed and skills to kick the ball over the try line and dive on it for the score. The try broke the Welsh try-scoring record: Shane was now the record holder. Stephen kicked the conversion and also a bit later on kicked a penalty to give us a 10-point cushion, but France were still looking dangerous. They were in a great scoring position with their scrum right on our line, but we managed to push them off their own ball and stop the danger, a major achievement in international rugby, especially in the context of that particular game and against a pack as good as the French had.

Dimitri Yachvili kicked a penalty but Stephen responded to keep the gap at 10 points, then Nugget picked the ball up from a ruck to run untouched under the posts for a try. We'd done it. We'd won the Grand Slam: the tenth time Wales had won it in their history and my first. Gats and the coaches had been in charge of only 5 games and we'd won them all, conceding only two tries in the whole tournament. Bringing Nugget back into the fold had been a huge success and an inspired move by Gats. What a turnaround we'd achieved in six months – really remarkable.

That summer we were going to be touring South Africa, playing two Tests. Prior to the tour, we had a week's training camp in Wexford, Ireland, where Gats and the coaches really put us through our paces. We were exposed for the first time to the cryotherapy chambers, where you're placed in a chamber for two and a half to three minutes in temperatures as low as -160° Celsius. The sensation's so hard to describe to somebody who hasn't experienced it, but the worst part's after you come out. You'd then spend 20 minutes on a cross trainer getting the blood flowing around your body again after the extremities of the chamber. It's brutal – after first session, a few players were vomiting outside. These temperatures allow your body to recover more quickly from the exertions of training, allowing us to train harder and faster the following day – as I said, it was brutal but it certainly worked. Gats wanted to make us the fittest and strongest team possible, and power and endurance were the areas we were really working on. We all wore GPS monitors so the coaches could track the distance we were running, speeds, etc., and after these sessions many of us were producing personal bests in strength and speed tests. Everyone's individual training requirements were then tailored around the output produced from the monitors we wore. We were getting superbly fit – right up there with the best international teams.

No stone was being left unturned – it was highly scientific. Gats believed strongly in rest periods: he trusted the players to know their own bodies, and if you wanted an afternoon away from weights and endurance then he was comfortable with that, but if he felt you weren't as fit or strong as you could be or as the others were, he and Shaun would let you know it and you put your position in the team and squad in real jeopardy. Players were made accountable.

At the training camp in Ireland, we were introduced to our new Conditioning Coach, Craig White. Craig had previously worked with London Wasps, Ireland and Leicester Tigers as well as the British and Irish Lions, and was another vital cog in our development as a rugby side. Craig would work alongside ex-Welsh international Mark Bennett, completing the coaching group. Gats wanted us to play the most outstanding teams in the world each year – New Zealand, Australia and South Africa: 'the big three', as he referred to them – to measure how good we were against the very best. In Gats' eyes, you had to play the best regularly to gauge your development as a player and as a team. Touring South Africa was going to be a big challenge, but we were Grand Slam winners and up to that challenge.

The first Test against South Africa was played in Bloemfontein and I got the start in the front row with Bomb and Melon either side. South Africa had a very strong team, as you'd expect, and they prided themselves on their pack of forwards and on being a strong set-piece side. Their front row that day was Brian Mujati, John Smit and Gurthrö Steenkamp, very strong boys. The scrum went really well for us, but we were outmuscled up front. We did score two tries through Jamie Roberts, who started at full back, and another from Shane Williams, but South Africa scored four and eventually came out on top 43 points to 17. Unfortunately, I picked up an injury and was replaced by Hibbs just after the 50-minute mark. After being examined, it was found that I'd torn my calf muscle. My tour was over and a few days later I was flying home to Wales.

In the second Test the following week in Pretoria we scored two tries through Gareth Cooper and Shane Williams but again South Africa scored four, winning 37 points to 21. From a Welsh perspective, the match is known for Jamie Roberts being asked to play at inside centre for the first time in his professional career. Shaun and Gats liked what he gave defensively and as a ball carrier, and with his size and ability to get over the gain line, he gave us another option. They identified this opportunity and, as we know, the rest is history. Jamie to that point had played full back and wing positions, but the inside centre position was to become his own for many years to come.

In the 2008 Autumn Series we played South Africa, Canada, New Zealand and Australia. In the game against South Africa we played well, with Andy Powell outstanding on his debut at his ball-carrying wrecking-ball best. Another debutant, Leigh Halfpenny, playing on the wing, also had a fine game and scored a try. We were in the game throughout but a few handling errors and poor decisions made under pressure cost us and we ended up losing to the Springboks by 20 points to 15. Against Canada, we got the victory but it was a disappointing performance overall. Halfpenny scored two tries and Dan Biggar came off the bench to gain his first cap, but we had a lot to work on for the big test in our next game, New Zealand.

My first encounter with New Zealand will always be remembered for what happened before the game: the infamous haka standoff. Many people have spoken and written about this event, but my memory is that Gats spoke to us about the tradition of the haka and how their challenge wasn't over until the opposition walked away after accepting the challenge. We asked the question: what would happen if we didn't walk away? What transpired was a great bit of drama, with referee Jonathan Kaplan finally asking both captains – Ryan Jones and Richie McCaw – to turn their teams around and go back to their respective halves to start the game. After quite a few minutes and with the fans going wild, when the referee intervened, both teams eventually went to their starting positions.

We led going into half-time, but the All Blacks stepped it up a few gears in the second half with Ma'a Nonu and Jerome Kaino scoring tries to ease away. Our response was three penalties from Stephen Jones, but the final score was Wales 9 New Zealand 29. Playing New Zealand for the first time was another special moment in my career, as was going head to head with Keven Mealamu, a fantastic player.

Our final game in the series was against Australia, and after defeats to South Africa and New Zealand already, Gats was desperate for us as a group to gain a victory. After only two minutes, Aussie captain Stirling Mortlock had to be replaced after a collision with Jamie Roberts. One minute later we scored a fantastic team try, through Shane yet again after a great pass from Gareth Cooper. Jamie Roberts lasted a bit longer before being replaced by Andrew Bishop – it turned out that Jamie had fractured his skull in the collision with Mortlock but had carried on playing – one tough bloke. Australia scored a long-range effort. In the second half, we scored a brilliant try from Byrney after Shane provided a great pass. Australia bounced back with a try and we were holding on at the end. Aussie fly half Matt Giteau failed with a late drop goal and we managed to hold on to gain the win by a scoreline of 21 points to 18. It was huge for us to gain a victory against a team from the

Southern Hemisphere, and our first win against Australia in 14 matches against them – a big boost in confidence and a win against one of the big three.

The 2009 Six Nations Championship was an opportunity for players to try to force their way into the upcoming summer tour, which was the small matter of the British and Irish Lions going to South Africa. Every player selected for any of the Home Nations in the tournament got fitted for Lions jerseys, shorts, etc., just in case they received the call-up. You do dare to dream a little bit at that point – you appreciate that you're still a long way away from being named in the squad, but if you get a decent run of games, who knows?

As reigning Champions, we started away at Scotland and after being behind, in the last ten minutes scored some late tries – further evidence of the improvement in our fitness. We scored four tries that day, from Shanks, AWJ, Leigh Halfpenny and Shane: a really promising start. Next up was England, and again we got the victory over a team struggling for confidence under the management of Martin Johnson. We scored a try through Leigh Halfpenny, who also kicked a penalty, and Stephen Jones was excellent, kicking five penalties and putting in a really commanding performance. England scored two tries of their own, so it was just as well that Stephen was on song. Two games into the tournament and two wins, and I had made two starts in a Lions year – all very positive!

Unfortunately though, in Paris our dreams of winning back-to-back Grand Slams for the first time since 1909 disintegrated. France deserve full credit for their victory. We didn't really get into our game at all and our normally solid defence let us down on a few occasions, especially with the Thierry Dusautoir try just before half-time, which was very poor defensively from us. We did get a narrow victory next up over Italy, before losing narrowly to Ireland at home, which meant Ireland winning the Grand Slam and the Six Nations Championship. We weren't firing on all cylinders during the tournament, but as the narrow defeats show, we weren't too far away. Ultimately though, to finish fourth one year after winning the Championship was very disappointing.

In the summer of 2009, Wales toured North America, where we took the opportunity to look at a few young players with a view to the World Cup in four years' time. Players such as Dan Lydiate, Jonathan Davies and a certain Sam Warburton all made an impression on that tour and showed Wales the potential they had and what players they'd be for their national side. That autumn we suffered defeats to New Zealand and Australia but gained victories against Samoa and Argentina. Overall though, I have to say that I felt that the year was a decline in performance from the heights of the previous year.

The 2010 Six Nations Championship started with England at Twickenham. I was unfortunately injured so Gareth Williams started, with Huw Bennett on the bench. The game was in the balance but after a yellow card for Alun Wyn, England scored 17 points. We did score two tries, one a rare effort from Bomb out wide on the wing and the other from Hooky, but England ran out worthy winners by 30 points to 17.

The following game was a classic against Scotland in Cardiff. Again, I was out due to injury and missed a great match. Scotland were up by 10 points with only 14 minutes to go, but with us putting more and more pressure on them, they picked up two yellow cards and ended up with only 13 men. A try from Shane in injury time after a number of phases of play meant we'd completed a fantastic comeback, winning by 31 points to 24. It was a great effort from the boys and coming back late on as they did showed the high levels of fitness within the squad that the coaches and players had been working on so diligently.

Going into the next round of games, France were looking very strong, having won their first two matches. Next they were coming to Cardiff. I was still out through injury and Gats went with Huw Bennett at hooker, with Ken Owens getting his first call-up to the squad as Gareth Williams was now also injured. The French raced into a 20 points to nil lead at half-time through tries by Alexis Palisson and François Trinh-Duc. We got back into the game through penalties by Stephen Jones and a try from Leigh Halfpenny, only for France to open up another gap via penalties by Frédéric Michalak. Shane scored yet another try right at the end but it wasn't enough. After a great game, we'd lost: the final score was Wales 20 France 26.

I managed to be fit for the trip to Ireland and got the start. Ireland were the reigning champions and a very good side – we were right in the game but a yellow card for Byrney was fully exploited by the Irish, who scored two tries whilst we were down to 14 men. Ireland really controlled the remainder of the game well and if Jonathan Sexton had had his kicking boots on, the gap could have been even wider. Final scoreline: Ireland 27 Wales 12.

We finished the campaign with a convincing victory at home against Italy, in a game in which Tom Prydie became the youngest ever international for Wales. Sam Warburton also got the start over Nugget and both players had impressive showings. Again we ended the competition in fourth place: it was poor, and for me personally, only playing in two of the five games due to injury was disappointing. I'd worked hard to become the first-choice hooker and had a number of players competing for the number 2 shirt, so missing games was giving others an opportunity to impress. I was desperate to be first choice for my country but I knew how tough the competition was in my position.

At the start of the Autumn Series several first-team players were missing due to injury: Byrney, Leigh, Jamie Roberts and our captain Ryan Jones. Gats had a number of players with leadership qualities in the squad who could replace Ryan as captain, such as Stephen Jones, Melon, Nugget and Alun Wyn. During the training camp for the game, we were in the indoor barn at the Vale when Gats approached me and as he walked by, asked me quite casually if I wanted to be captain in the match against Australia, adding that if I didn't, he'd get someone else. The question caught me completely by surprise but I didn't hesitate, and said yes! The manner in which Gats asked the question was typical of him: no frills, he just came out and asked. I couldn't believe it – I was going to captain my country. Even though I knew Ryan would likely be back the following week to regain the captaincy, it was a huge honour.

Leading the side out onto the pitch for the first time was very emotional for me and my family, and an experience I'll never forget. Standing there singing the anthem as captain is very, very special and something that will stay with me forever. In the game itself we had a lot of joy in the scrum, where we dominated Australia, but when they had the ball in hand they constantly made inroads into our defence and scored three tries in the game. We did score a consolation try from scrum half Richie Rees, but were defeated by 25 points to 16. The result was disappointing even if we were missing a few of our stars – overall, to lose again to a Southern Hemisphere side showed there was still work required with a World Cup only one year away.

The following weekend we faced South Africa. As it turned out, Ryan was fit to start only on the bench so I retained the captaincy, but we lost Dan Lydiate and Melon to injury very late on before the match – two key losses. We did, however, have Byrney and Nugget fit and back in the side, as well as a young winger making his first appearance for Wales: George North. George had a great debut, scoring two tries – one from his first touch in international rugby! Everything he did, he looked completely at home on the international stage. We led for large periods of the game but South Africa came back, and two tries plus 19 points from the boot of Morné Steyn got them a narrow victory by 29 points to 25. We'd now won one game in our last 11 internationals, a statistic that made for damning reading. We were regularly pushing top sides to narrow losses so we could see improvements within the group, but the results didn't lie: we were coming up short.

Fiji were next up and Gats made a few changes to the starting line-up. Huw Bennett started at hooker, with Richard Hibbard as his back-up, and Ryan Jones was also back as captain. The performance from the side wasn't up to expected standards and we came away with a draw. After the game, Gats and the coaches were livid about the team's performance and a few choice words were given to the players. One statement Gats made in the heat of the moment was to tell all of us that for the next game, against New Zealand, I was going to be captain.

I remember that Gats confirmed on the Monday of the week building up to the game that I was indeed going to be captain – Ryan was now fit, but Gats was standing by his decision after the Fiji game. I called a meeting with the players, and asked them what we needed to get out of the week to give us the best chance against New Zealand. Not that any of us have fared very well against them, mind! I just felt I needed to speak to others who I respected to make sure I wasn't missing anything, which for a new captain is natural, really.

Captaining your country is very special and captaining them against New Zealand is right up there as a highlight of my career. The game was a great battle. Late in the game we were close to them, with Stephen kicking six penalties, but then – as often happens – New Zealand pulled away, scoring two additional tries. Byrney did score a consolation try but it was too little, too late – another loss to the All Blacks. Three games against Australia, South Africa and New Zealand and we'd lost all three. Were we going to be competitive in the World Cup the following year? Gats certainly believed we could be – was he right?

CHAPTER 9

The Highs and Lows

2011 WAS WORLD Cup year and preparations had long been underway to give us the best chance of being as successful as possible. Before the World Cup kicked off, there was the small matter of a Six Nations tournament to go through and first up was England in Cardiff, with me leading the team out. I couldn't wait. Gats had said in the press in the week building up to the game that my direct opponent, Dylan Hartley, was a weak link, which certainly generated some column inches in the papers and got people talking. Gats likes a bit of controversy from time to time to get people's backs up and to give them something else to talk about rather than just the match itself – it's all part of the game for him.

The game against England was, as always, tough and we were trailing by 14 points going into the final quarter. Then we scored a try through Morgan Stoddart, who was playing on the wing, the try being converted by Stephen Jones. Hooky then scored a penalty, leaving us only four points back, but Johnny Wilkinson kicked a penalty to seal the victory for them. The first game at home in the Six Nations, and losing to England wasn't the start any of us wanted. Next up was away to Scotland: another big challenge.

Against Scotland, we played very well. We led through a Shane Williams try which was converted by Hooky, who also scored three penalties. We then went down to thirteen players in a matter of two minutes, Byrney and Bradley Davies taking the ten-minute breaks. However, despite both of them being off the pitch, we only conceded three points through the boot of Dan Parks – yet another example of how good our defence was and how well drilled we were by Shaun Edwards. Shane scored another try later on and we ran out convincing winners, which is never easy at Murrayfield.

We had another away game next up: in Rome against Italy. In a game with many twists and turns, we came out on top after two tries, one from Morgan Stoddart and the other from Sam Warburton – his first international try. Warbs had a fine game and was showing how good a player he was at international level. The back row – him, Dan Lydiate and Ryan Jones – was working really well, as were a number of combinations, which gave us a lot of confidence. We'd won two away games on the bounce and next were Ireland in Cardiff.

The Irish led at half-time and Brian O'Driscoll had scored a try, putting him equal with the record for tries in the history of the Championship. The game is remembered for the Mike Phillips try where I took a throw-in to the front and Mike peeled around to run away for the score; however, the try is remembered for the fact that the line-out was taken with the wrong ball – not the ball that was cleared into touch by Johnny Sexton. Not something we'd practised on the training field, believe me. The officials missed it and the try stood, and we held on late in the game to take another victory. With one game left away to France, we had a chance of winning the Championship.

We had to beat France by 27 points to win the Championship. Before the game, we talked about not worrying too much about the scoreboard initially – concentrating on getting the win and then revaluating once the game was won before trying to push the scoreline. France had lost to Italy in their previous game so a backlash was a worry. Prior to kick-off, Gats again gained publicity by saying the French pack weren't as fit as they could be. Gats has made this type of comment prior to matches many times, and more often than not it's for our benefit rather than to get at the opposition – as in, to say I believe you're fitter and stronger than them and you should gain confidence from this: believe in yourselves.

In the game itself, the French were far better in the first half, Lionel Nallet scoring two tries. Early in the game, Warbs was injured and had to be replaced, which meant Dan Lydiate moving to openside and Jonathan Thomas coming on at blindside flanker. This did mean a few adjustments, but it's no excuse. We did play far better in the second half, but another French try from Vincent Clerc saw them win convincingly. Due to how the final round of matches went, England ended up winning the Championship with France in second and Ireland third. We, France and Ireland all ended up on the same number of points, but points difference left us in fourth.

The players had planned a catch-up after the Six Nations – an event we called 'Super Sunday'. After the Six Nations and Autumn Series finished, players were normally given a few days off to recover, so on the Sunday we would get together for a few beers. We'd start at the Vale, where the fridges were full of booze, ready for the event. After slipping from second to fourth, I decided to cancel this as it was felt that it may not look good if Welsh rugby fans saw us out 'celebrating'. However, a few players decided still to go out, which I found out about from Team Manager Alan Phillips. Thumper (as he's known in rugby circles) wasn't impressed and wanted me to talk to them as captain. I did so after the event, to make them think about how fans would react to that kind of thing.

Even though we finished fourth in the Championship, I felt really confident that we'd have a successful World Cup. It was going to be my second World Cup and I was going to captain my country. I was so looking forward to it: I really believed this group could do something special. We had a pool of players who'd been together for a few years and who were at the peak of their playing powers. We had a great mix of youth and experience and South Africa, who were in our group, were a team we'd pushed close a few times recently. We were always looking to peak at the tournament.

Prior to the World Cup, we went to Spala in Poland for intense training sessions including the infamous cryotherapy chambers (previously mentioned), with temperatures as low as -160° Celsius, to speed up physical recovery. The sessions were brutal: up at 6 a.m., train, then breakfast and then weights, and back to the cryo chambers. We'd travelled to Poland prior to the 2011 Six Nations as well, but the difference for me was that on this second visit I was able to do hardly any weights. I was really struggling and was becoming increasingly concerned about my participation in the World Cup.

I had suffered a neck injury just before the end of the League season with the Scarlets. The physio looked over the injury and a decision was made that the injury would settle and I could get through the World Cup and have the operation when the tournament ended. As a professional sportsman you trust the physio's expertise, and I became more hopeful. However, whilst in Poland I was involved in meetings with Gats and Thumper, talking about functions that I as the captain needed to attend during the World Cup. Hearing about those, knowing the discomfort I was in and fearing I wouldn't be there in New Zealand, made me feel even worse, but I didn't say anything as I still held out hope. I was rooming with Melon and some nights I couldn't sleep due to the pain I was in. I was losing feeling in my hands and constantly feeling sick, and I knew that I was highly doubtful to make the upcoming World Cup. I was just not myself due to the pain, and the coaches could see I was a different person and really struggling.

On the way back from Poland, I went to Bristol to have my neck examined. The results of the examination weren't a surprise to me at all at that point: I needed to have an operation to remove 50% of a disc from my neck to relieve the pressure. I'd be missing the World Cup and the opportunity to captain my country. I was gutted. I gave the coaches the bad news, and felt so down about it all. Before I went into the hospital, to try to get over the disappointment I had a family holiday with Becky and Brooke to Disneyland Paris, but I regularly had to disappear to find the nearest toilet to be sick. By the end, I knew where every toilet in Disneyland was. It was pretty miserable for me, but the other two seemed to enjoy the holiday, luckily!

When we got back, I went under the knife in Bristol to have my neck fixed and not long after having the operation and whilst still on the ward, I took an unexpected call from Gats. He explained that he'd just offered the World Cup captaincy role to Warbs, who didn't want to take it on. Gats asked if I could speak to Warbs to see if he'd reconsider. I was very surprised that Gats had offered the role to Warbs – I thought he'd have gone with Melon or Alun Wyn – but the more I thought about it, the more sense it made. Gats already knew he had leaders in his team such as the two I've mentioned, but he wanted a player who was guaranteed a starting spot, a really hard-working player who just got on with things. He also wanted to bring a new leader through, and Warbs fitted the bill for him.

At the time I wasn't that close to Warbs. Apart from seeing him in the Welsh squad and playing alongside him, I didn't know him that well as a person. Sam was still reasonably new to international rugby and he spent most of his time hanging around with Dan Lydiate and Toby Faletau – the back row was as close off the field as they were on it! What I did know was that even after that short time, he was well respected within the group and liked.

I contacted Warbs and explained that Gats had asked me to phone, and asked him why he'd turned the job down. Warbs said that he felt it was just too early for him. He hadn't captained at a regional level and didn't feel that he was at a level of enough seniority in the squad to take the position. My advice to him was simple: that he had enough respect in the group and that an opportunity like this doesn't come around often. I told him that I hadn't been sure if I was ready to be captain when I was offered the role, but with great support around you over time you start to feel more comfortable in the role. Warbs said he'd think about it and as we all know now, the rest is history. Wales went on to reach the semi-finals in a great World Cup and Warbs has been a captain respected around the sporting world. Personally, missing that World Cup is the biggest disappointment in my rugby career – being captain of my national side in a World Cup would for me have been the ultimate accolade. I was proud watching them out there, but it was still painful to watch as I kept thinking that it could have been me playing as captain of Wales in a World Cup semi-final – but it wasn't to be.

I was back playing ten weeks after the operation, which was a great success. Due to my absence, I was unfortunately not on the field for Shane Williams' last game for Wales – against Australia in the 2011 Autumn Series. It was a game that ultimately we lost, but Shane scored his 58th try for Wales, an unbelievable record which may never be broken. Shane was a special rugby talent and you knew if you could remain in games with him on the pitch, you always had a chance. After my injury I was ready, if asked, to be back in the squad for the 2012 Six Nations. Prior to the tournament, we were again in Poland for a training programme, but this time in Gdansk, which at least wasn't in the middle of nowhere like Spala. I made the journey as part of the squad for the upcoming tournament and I was delighted to be back in the fold, even though I knew that the training was going to be brutal, which again it was.

Dublin was the location for the first game, which I wasn't part of due to a calf injury. It was a great match, with both teams playing brilliant rugby. We managed to gain a narrow victory through a last-minute penalty by Leigh Halfpenny, after three earlier tries through Foxy (with two) and George North. We then soundly beat Scotland through a home debut try from Alex Cuthbert and two tries from Leigh Halfpenny, who scored 22 of the 27 Wales points in the game. We'd be going to Twickenham in search of a Triple Crown. Having also missed the Scottish game through injury, I was desperate to be back for the England match.

Sadly, I wasn't ready and didn't play a part in the Triple Crown game, with Hibbs starting and Ken Owens as the cover at hooker. The game was really close and was locked at 12 points all, through penalties by Leigh for us and Owen Farrell for them. With five minutes left, replacement Scott Williams turned the ball over by ripping it from the hands of Courtney Lawes on halfway, grubber kicking it ahead and gathering it to score: really a great individual effort. Right at the end, David Strettle almost got over in the corner only for our defence to stop the opposition. We'd won the Triple Crown at Twickenham.

I started the next game at home to Italy. Gats also brought in Justin Tipuric for Warbs with Melon taking the captaincy. Many thought that I'd be given the captaincy with Warbs missing and me starting, but Gats wanted me to concentrate on my own game and Melon had been captain on a number of occasions. I had no issue at all with this decision – I was just happy to be selected. Italy were very tough to break down initially, but then we moved away with tries from Jamie Roberts and Alex Cuthbert and kicks from Leigh and Rhys Priestland. We'd won four from four, one game away from the Grand Slam.

In addition to being able to secure us the Grand Slam, the French game was also my fiftieth appearance for Wales, a number I never dreamed I'd reach. Warbs, who was back to captain the side, picked up a shoulder injury and had to be replaced by Ryan Jones. It was a hugely physical encounter throughout: both sets of players were laying everything on the line and some of the hits going in, especially from Thierry Dusautoir and Dan Lydiate, were immense to see up close. We scored a try through Alex Cuthbert and managed to get ourselves over the line. We'd won the Grand Slam. The preparations Gats and the coaches had put in had worked, we were immensely fit and our defence was fantastic. Each player knew their role and after a great World Cup, we were now the Six Nations Champions again. It was such a proud moment, and personally it was great to play in the last two games and feel I'd done my bit. I was over the moon to be part of a Grand

Slam-winning side and, as Becky reminds me, it was the first time I ever acknowledged her existence in the crowd after the game by waving to her, so I must have been happy!

That summer we toured Australia, led by Robert Howley. Gats had been asked to be Head Coach of the British and Irish Lions tour the following year and would take a break from coaching Wales to enable him to visit the other international sides, keep an eye on players, etc. Before we toured Australia, Wales had a game against Barbarians in Cardiff and with players missing, I was asked again to captain the side, an honour I was more than happy to take on. The game was given full international status, meaning that caps would be awarded. This meant Nugget would gain his one-hundredth appearance for Wales, a fantastic achievement and fully deserved by someone who gave so much for his country – simply a superb player. Also on that day full international debuts were made by Harry Robinson, Rhodri Jones and Liam Williams, and Adam Warren also came off the bench to earn a cap. We won the game by 30 points to 21. The Baa-Baas had a very decent side out and it was very strange to be in opposition to Shane Williams and Richie Rees, who were wearing the famous black and white hooped jersey, after playing with both for Wales.

For the first Test in Brisbane, Howlers went with Ken Owens to start with myself on the bench, a decision that I wasn't too surprised by as Ken was in fine form and I hadn't trained properly due to a small niggling injury. I came on after 51 minutes to replace Ken – we were losing and even though Alex Cuthbert scored a try and Leigh knocked over a few penalties, it wasn't enough to gain the victory and Australia won by 27 points to 19.

For the second Test, I got the start with Hibbs this time selected to be on the bench. If we were going to win the Test series, we had to win this one, and we started really well with George North scoring a try after four minutes. I came off with ten minutes to play, being replaced by Hibbs. Unfortunately, Hibbs conceded two penalties in that period – we were leading throughout the game until Mike Harris for Australia kicked a penalty right at the last minute to take the win by 25 points to 23. We were so deflated afterwards. When we had a video review of the previous game in the week building up to the next Test, Hibbs had to deal with some probing questions from the coaches over the penalties he'd conceded, and they also questioned his choice of white footwear as it made it easier for match officials to spot if he was slightly offside or on the wrong side at a ruck, etc. After such a disappointing end to the previous match, we were determined that we'd get some pride back by taking the final Test the following week.

For the third and final Test, I got the start but this time Ken was on the bench. Again, we were leading after a Ryan Jones try and Halfpenny being deadly from the tee. Unfortunately, again, Australia got the win by 20 points to 19, a late penalty from Berrick Barnes this time being the decider. We'd lost all three Tests by a total points difference of eleven, and only three points over the last two Tests. Such small margins, but to be a top international side you need to win out in these tight games and we knew we had a lot to learn.

Our first autumn international was against Argentina, who were excellent. We didn't perform as we should have, but people still underestimate how good Argentina had become as an international side. They'd pushed New Zealand in the quarter-final of the World Cup only the year before, and were far better in this match, scoring two tries to our none and running out 26 points to 12 winners. Howlers and the players were all under pressure now that we'd lost four internationals on the bounce after winning a Grand Slam. Next up were Samoa, a team who'd surprised us before. It couldn't happen again, could it?

For the Samoan game, Howlers went with Hibbs to start and Ken as the replacement, so I was watching in the stands. What I saw was painful. Samoa were superior in all facets of the game. They scored three tries and we only scored the one, following a long-range interception try from Ashley Beck. Losing to Samoa for the third time caused a huge backlash from fans and media alike. This was our fifth loss on the trot: these losses now affected our World rankings for the next World Cup, and people doubted whether Howlers was the right man to coach us in Gats' absence. I did feel sorry for Howlers, who was caught in all this fury. From a training perspective, there'd been little change – we were simply not performing. Some in the media believed that Gats was still selecting the side and coming up with the training plan, etc., but as a player I never saw any real evidence of this. From what I saw, Howlers was calling the shots. We were all up against it and next up were New Zealand – not what you want when you aren't performing and are under pressure.

For the New Zealand game we did have Gats back leading us, during a break with the Lions. I got the nod to start at hooker to face the most challenging team in rugby. We played reasonably well on the day, scoring two tries through Scott Williams and Alex Cuthbert. However, New Zealand were just too strong, scoring three tries of their own, including a fantastic one by Liam Messam after a mesmerising break from Israel Dagg and Julian Savea in the build-up. We did have a number of injuries going into the game so had players absent, but that's no excuse – New Zealand were simply too good.

The final game of the autumn was against one of our most frequent adversaries by this point, Australia. I got the start and we were all determined to get the victory and not leave this series empty-handed. We played well and were leading with only a minute left following four penalties from Leigh Halfpenny, who had an outstanding game. Australia made a break, with Dave Dennis feeding Kurtley Beale, who dived over for the winning try, evading a desperate dive from Alex Cuthbert. We'd lost again to Australia by less than three points – the third time in a year this had happened. After the game and losing to them again, I felt sick. It was just a horrible feeling. Seven international losses on the bounce after being Grand Slam winners – we all collectively had to take responsibility and turn this around.

For the start of the Six Nations we faced Ireland, and by half-time we were looking at a hammering – down by 20 points. We did come back in the second half to make it a real competition, but ultimately fell short. Next up was France in Paris and I wasn't selected, Howlers going with Hibbs and Ken as his back-up. I did ask Howlers about this, as though I accept we'd lost to Ireland in the opening game and hadn't performed in the first half, the only starting players from that match who missed out were me, Aaron Shingler and (due to injury) Warbs. I felt I'd played well enough to keep my place, and told Howlers this. He said that he wanted to see Hibbs get a start and liked Ken as an impact option off the bench. Both are good players, but I felt I deserved to play. I had a feeling (and still do) that at that point, Hibbs was being considered for the British and Irish Lions tour that summer, so they wanted him to gain some international starts to see how he went prior to the tour, and this is why I missed out.

As it turned out, Wales beat France, with Leigh Halfpenny yet again outstanding. Wales then went on to beat Italy and Scotland and score a fantastic victory against England in Cardiff by 30 points to 3 – when we were totally dominant, playing some great rugby – meaning we won the Championship. Hibbs was outstanding, especially against England – with some huge hits in defence – and also scored a try against Scotland. He did indeed show he deserved inclusion with the British and Irish Lions, but being dropped after the Ireland game did hurt as I didn't feel it was warranted.

I've loved my time playing for my country, with all the highs and lows you get when playing for nine years. I've had the privilege of being coached by some excellent coaches, but Gats in particular, who made me captain and always treated me very well and with honesty, is an outstanding coach who I owe an awful lot to.

CHAPTER 10

It's a Family Affair

As I mentioned in the first chapter, I was brought up by my mum as a single parent with support from close family members. I mentioned as well that my dad, Paul, wasn't a big part of my childhood with only infrequent visits – once a week, on Wednesdays – and cards and money for events such as birthdays and Christmas. However, the true story behind my family life only came out much later.

I discovered in my teens that Paul wasn't in fact my dad, and only found out who my biological father was when I was 20 and playing for Pontypridd. For anyone, something like that's a huge shock and a real life changer. It's a story that few apart from family and close friends have known.... that is, until now.

Before I came along, my mum was married to Paul, who comes from Cardiff. They had two children but split up a few years later and my mum moved to Tonyrefail with my sister Lisa and my brother Martin to be closer to her family, who lived in the area. I can remember in my early childhood spending some time with Paul, but around the age of 8 or 9 these visits stopped and my only contact was by birthday/Christmas cards signed 'To Matthew. Lots of love, Dad'. During this time my mum had a fourth child, Julian, so we were a reasonably big family, with three boys and one girl.

When I was 11 years old, my mum started dating a man called Wayne. He used to take me to rugby training and also came with Mum to watch some of my games at Tonyrefail. As we had this common bond of rugby, I really got on with Wayne. He never lived with us, but was always around if I needed him and we had a good relationship. Wayne owned a pub later on, and unfortunately ended up dying relatively young after becoming addicted to drink. Being around alcohol all day, Wayne had got more and more into the drinking scene, which ultimately led to his demise. I attended his funeral and it was all very sad that he passed so young.

When I reached the age of 13, birthday cards from my dad stopped, which I found very strange. When I quizzed my mum, she just said he could be forgetful with dates, which for a young lad made little sense, but I just accepted it. I never really had a father figure in my life growing up, with the exception of the short period with Wayne, and my Uncle Dave. I have a lot to thank my uncle for over the years.

As years passed and I was getting older and more confident in my own mind and about what I wanted, and with things not being great at home with my mum, I decided I was going to speak to this man called Paul Rees who I still believed was my dad, and get some questions answered.

I managed to get his number and phoned him. I just wanted to have a relationship with him so asked to meet up, not just because he was my dad but also due to the fact that my relationship with my mum was so poor at the time. His response was one I'll never forget, as he calmly told me over the phone in a very matter-of-fact manner that he wasn't my dad, and that for more information I should speak to my grandparents. To say I was stunned is an understatement. I was angry, upset and a number of emotions flowed through me. If he was telling the truth, then who was my dad? I did as Paul suggested and spoke to my grandparents, who said, 'Go and speak to your mum.' They knew who my dad was but, and I do understand this, felt that the information should be coming from my mum rather than from them. When I spoke to Mum and told her I now knew that Paul wasn't my dad, she wouldn't tell me who it was. I was so angry that night that I stayed at my uncle and auntie's house. My uncle and auntie also knew the truth but they, like my grandparents, felt that news of this magnitude should come from her.

My relationship with my mum deteriorated. I just wanted to know the truth about who my dad was. We'd go for long periods without speaking because I was so frustrated and angry. With rugby I was able to forget about what was going on and take my frustrations out on the pitch, but that was only for fleeting moments of time, and then the anger and hurt would return.

This carried on for a few years, with still no further information. When I was playing with Pontypridd U21s and Treorchy, I moved in with my girlfriend (later to be my wife) Becky, who was living on her own. A couple more years elapsed and then around Christmas time, Becky went out for a family meal which my auntie and grandmother were also at. After some time had passed and a few drinks had been had, my auntie asked Becky if I had much contact with my father. My grandmother quickly nudged her to make her realise what she'd said, and tried to change the subject, but Becky replied to my auntie, "How can he be in touch with his dad when he doesn't know who his dad is?" The subject swiftly changed but at the end of the night when Becky came back to the house we shared, she told me what had happened. At this point it was obvious to us both that people did know who my dad was. We both decided that night that this time I wasn't going to allow this to continue, I was going to find out who he was – the not knowing was too painful now.

I spoke to my uncle and explained to him what had happened with my auntie. I know my auntie hadn't meant to drop anyone in it and felt terrible about the conversation she'd had with Becky. It wasn't her fault – she thought I knew, but it raised the subject yet again and this time I was determined not to let it go as I had on other occasions. Eventually my uncle cracked and finally confessed that he believed my dad was a man called Ken who owned a TV shop in the village, and said that I should speak to my mum again to get this confirmed. My relationship with my mum was poor at the time so I decided I wouldn't approach the subject immediately. A few months passed with this constant thought about who my dad was festering away in my head. Eventually, after a night out when I'd had a few beers, I went back to see my uncle to discuss the matter again, and the next day I went to confront my mum with what I'd been told. I said that if she didn't tell me the truth, I'd speak to Ken myself. Finally, my mum gave me the information I'd wanted to hear for so many years: my dad was indeed a man who'd lived in the village all the time, and my uncle was correct. Ken had owned the TV shop for as long as I can remember, and the remarkable thing is that I'd walked past that shop every day on my way to and from school, and for all those years inside that shop was my dad! I was 20 years of age and finally I knew who my biological father was. I was desperate to know more and to ask questions, and my mum promised to speak to Ken to see whether he wanted to meet up. Fortunately, he agreed and it was arranged that the three of us would all meet up to talk through the situation.

The day I met up with my dad, I was a nervous wreck. We met at his house, where he lived alone (and still does), and he gave me more of the story that I was desperate to know. He and my mum had had a brief relationship whilst he was married. He'd always believed that he was my dad and had seen me around the village. He'd reached out to my mum a few times, asking if he was my dad, and had been told that he wasn't, but deep down he'd always believed he was. He told me that he'd admitted to the affair to his then wife. On hearing the news, his wife had left him, taking their 15-year-old son Simon with her, leaving him all alone. My dad hadn't seen Simon since they moved out, but had written to him a few times. On finding out about me, he wrote to Simon to explain that he had a brother and after some time had passed Simon wrote back and we've met up a few times since. I struggled, and continue to struggle, to understand why, if he believed I was his son, he hadn't done more to contact me. I also struggle with the decision my mum made not to tell me for all those years who my dad was. Her dad (my grandfather) told her, after Paul stopped coming around to visit me, to tell me who my real dad was, but she refused. She believed she was protecting me, but I don't see it that way. I often think about what would I do in their position, and I do believe I'd have dealt with it completely differently. But you can't go back in time: what happened happened.

I have a good relationship now with my dad and see him frequently, trying to catch up on the time we lost. I also live quite close to my mum and again, I'm in regular contact. It must not have been easy bringing up four children on her own. Money was tight and we didn't have summer holidays – though we did have the odd day trip away – but for birthdays and at Christmas she always had presents for us all, taking out a loan with Provident each time and paying them back weekly. As a junior playing rugby, a few times I had to put tape around my rugby boots to hold them together, to get them through to the end of the season. Even though I feel some things could have been handled differently, it must have been very challenging and I know she did her best.

When I look back over my childhood there are a lot of 'what if?'s about how different my upbringing could have been if my dad had been on the scene throughout. One conclusion I've come to is that if I'd known earlier who my real dad was, I'd have changed my surname. The name Rees doesn't mean a great deal to me, as it isn't who I am. I'm carrying the surname on, as are Becky and Brooke, but it all feels a bit absurd. My real dad's surname is Gay – I'm sure the less enlightened in the crowd would have had a field day, seeing that emblazoned on the back of my rugby shirt! However, to be honest, the surname I'd have taken would have been Edgecombe, my mum's maiden name. As Rees is now my wife and daughter's surname, I wouldn't change it now, but – not to offend my mum and dad, but just being honest – now knowing who my biological dad is, the name isn't a real representation of who I am.

All in all, my childhood was challenging, but there are children who have far worse upbringings than my brothers and sister and I had. As a boy struggling with my emotions, rugby was an escape for me, and I was thankful that it was a big part of my life even back then.

CHAPTER 11

Becoming a Lion

AT THE BEGINNING of April 2009, I was travelling to Llanelli to play for the Scarlets against Glasgow when I received a call from Rob Howley. Howlers just wanted to let me know that certain people linked to the upcoming British and Irish Lions Tour would be watching that night, so he advised me to 'do what you do well', like set pieces, etc., as basically it was between me and another hooker (who he didn't name) as to who'd be on the plane going to South Africa with the Lions.

When I hung up, I did feel a little bit more nervous than I had prior to the conversation! Being chosen as a Lion is the ultimate accolade for a rugby player, and here I was being told I was very much in the mix to become part of that exclusive group. We lost to Glasgow that night, unfortunately, but I did feel my own performance went quite well. I just had to hope that this performance and others before and after would be enough to get me into that squad.

Did I think before that telephone call that I'd be in the squad? Well, I thought I was good enough, but I appreciated how many good players I was up against in my position in the UK and Ireland. Players such as Lee Mears, Dylan Hartley, Jerry Flannery, Rory Best, Ross Ford and Huw Bennett all had a great chance to tour. Having Gats and Howlers involved in the coaching group going to South Africa could work in my favour, and I was reasonably pleased with how I'd done in the previous Six Nations, which is always a showcase for an upcoming British and Irish Lions tour. However, Ireland going so well and winning the Championship must have been good for their players' prospects. Another advantage in terms of getting into the squad where there are some close calls is to be playing in the latter stages of European competitions, pitting your skills against the very best. In conclusion, I knew it was going to be close – I just had to hope what I could offer as a player would be enough.

As is the way nowadays, the squad announcement was made live on Sky Sports in mid-April. The names were read out by the Tour Manager for the British and Irish Lions, legendary rugby figure Gerald Davies, who announced the names in alphabetical order by surname. As he was going through the names, I was with the rest of the Scarlets squad in the meeting room prior to training in Llanelli, and a big cheer went up when Stephen Jones was announced. I was listening intently and I knew I'd have a wait with my surname! When Gerald with his smooth Welsh tones said the name Matthew Rees, I was relieved and elated – I was going to be a Lion. The boys congratulated me and Stephen and just before we went out to training, Paul Moriarty (who was taking the session) said if I wanted to sit the training out after hearing that news, he'd totally understand. I was on cloud nine but I told him I wanted to train. If I'm honest, the training's all a bit of a blur – my head was spinning: I was going to be a Lion!

When we finished training, I checked my mobile phone and saw I had lots of missed calls and plenty of text messages wishing me luck and congratulations from friends and family. When I got home, Becky, my auntie and uncle and I went out for a meal as a celebration after the great news. I couldn't wait to meet up with the squad and be part of the Lions tradition. The other hookers named to tour were Jerry Flannery of Munster and Ireland and Lee Mears of Bath and England. In my head, Jerry was probably leading the hunt for the Test hooker shirt, then Lee and then me, but on a 10-match tour, who knows what could happen. As we've seen many times on previous tours and will no doubt see again, the favourite for a certain spot doesn't always end up with the jersey, due to numerous circumstances.

The touring squad all met up for a week in Pennyhill Park in Surrey. The Welsh players who'd been named – all 14 of us – travelled up from the Vale together with Tommy Bowe, who was playing for the Ospreys at the time. Ian McGeechan talked to us about the challenge we were facing and the honour of playing for the Lions, and the passion he spoke with about what we now were part of – this exclusive group – made the hairs on the back of my neck stand up. It was a skill he demonstrated many times over on that tour. After the criticism levelled at the 2005 New Zealand tour, Geech was determined that the Lions were going back to basics. There'd be just one group: team togetherness was vital and we'd participate in a lot of events together and share rooms with a number of different players over the duration of the tour so as to get to know each other. All of which worked really well with this group of players.

The coaching group we had with us was outstanding. It was led by Geech, but Gats was there as forwards coach, Howlers as attack coach, Graham Rowntree as scrummaging coach, Shaun Edwards as defence coach and Neil Jenkins as kicking coach – a great unit with loads of experience. We also had Craig White as fitness coach, so the team included a number of coaches I'd worked with before with Wales. Especially with Geech and Graham, two coaches I admired, I was really looking forward to being trained by them and to seeing the playing style we'd adopt. South Africa pride themselves on their forward play so we knew we'd have to be strong in that department – Gats and Rowntree had their work cut out to make sure we were a match for them up front.

The first week in Pennyhill was intense. We had to endure altitude chambers to help us acclimatise to the conditions we'd face in South Africa, which are always tough. We also had a lot of sessions working on specific skills and going through some generic playing patterns, set-piece sessions, etc. South Africa had won the World Cup only two years earlier and those players were still playing, ready to face the Lions. Their pack was massive and crammed with top players and we knew the challenge we had to face. That week in Pennyhill, I roomed with Joe Worsley, who was great – as were the others I shared with through the tour, such as Donncha O'Callaghan, Simon Shaw, Luke Fitzgerald, Rob Kearney, Stephen Ferris and Phil Vickery. Good lads, each and every one of them.

As I said, the training was tough that first week. After only a few days Jerry Flannery got injured, and unfortunately had to pull out of the tour. Jerry was replaced by Ross Ford of Edinburgh and Scotland, another top player, and instantly the starting hooker spot opened up. A number of the originally named squad ended up being unavailable, some due to injuries picked up playing for their clubs prior to the squad meeting up (such as Shanks and Tomás O'Leary). Injuries also happen on tour, and this tour would be no different – it was brutal at times. After training we spent time socialising and getting acquainted with players from other countries we may not have known so well. Paul O'Connell was our captain – a colossus of a player and a great leader. Being there with all these fantastic players from the other home nations, as well as my Welsh teammates such as Melon, Bomb, Nugget, Byrney, AWJ and Mike Phillips, amongst others, was very special. I was humbled and still couldn't believe that I was part of this group of amazing players. As I mentioned, training was tough, but there was time for some socialising. An example of how well we got on is that on the Wednesday night we all met up in the bar for a few drinks as a squad. The following day there were activities planned, but seeing that we'd stayed in the bar till 5.30 in the morning drinking, those activities were postponed!

The coaches decided that they'd name the side to start the first game a few days before we travelled to South Africa, to allow us to work on set pieces, defensive patterns, combinations, etc. I was delighted to find out that I'd be starting the first game in the famous Lions red shirt. Geech and the other coaches made it clear to us all that we'd all get a start before the first Test so as to show them what we could do, and they were true to their word. On the last day in Pennyhill, players' and coaches' families were invited to join us for a few drinks and a meal and to spend some quality time before we left for South Africa. We'd be gone from our families for six weeks so it was a lovely gesture to allow us that time. Brooke was nearly two at the time, and it was special to share this moment with her and Becky before going away with the Lions.

Just before the first game on tour in Rustenburg, Andy Powell, who'd been selected, pulled out with a hand injury. It's a shame for any player not to be able to play when selected, as you're desperate to make your mark and show the coaches what you can do. We got the victory against Royal XV and a few days after the game, the players had the opportunity to enjoy a golfing day, which I jumped at. Lo and behold, who also put his name down for a day of golf but Powelly! I think it's fair to say, after that the coaches weren't too sure how bad his hand really was if he was able to swing a golf club for 18 holes only a few days later! Powelly's a hell of a character and on the thirteenth tee on that golfing day, I turned round to see him doing muscle poses shirtless on top of a golf buggy. This obviously reminds me of another story of Powelly and a golf buggy the following year, which you may have heard about. Powelly's a fantastic guy to have around the squad on tour – he's an absolute scream and when on form was a fantastic rugby player, creating havoc with his ball-carrying abilities.

A Lions tour isn't just about the playing side of things. It involves travelling around the country visiting schools, attending functions, doing corporate events and spreading the great game of rugby through the British and Irish Lions brand. The planning prior to the corporate events was that those players who'd been selected to play in the coming days wouldn't attend – those not selected would take on the responsibilities to allow the players the opportunity to prepare

– and it worked really well. Other than that, we stayed together as a group throughout the tour, unlike other tours I've heard about where there was a definite split between the Test team and the midweek team. The only time that the group was split and in different parts of the country was midweek before the first Test, when many players travelled to play Southern Kings in Port Elizabeth and the others stayed back to prepare for the first Test. As that was being played in Durban only three days later, it made perfect sense to divide up for that short period.

In the first six games we played prior to the first Test we were unbeaten, defeating teams such as Free State Cheetahs, the Sharks and Western Province – all quality sides. We were building nicely in preparation for the Tests and were optimistic. The matches were already very tough and we lost a number of players to injury before the first Test, with replacements needed to come out to reinforce the squad. They all did a great job. Personally, I was pleased with how things were going; I was getting plenty of game time and going by the selections, it appeared to be between me and Lee Mears for the hooker slot. Lee was a good player, busy around the field and a good ball-carrier, so I just had my fingers crossed I'd get the Test shirt. It would be a dream come true.

The first Test team was announced on the Tuesday evening and then we went out for food together. I'd made the Test match-day squad, which was pleasing, but had to make do with a place on the bench, with Lee Mears getting the nod at hooker. Melon was starting so I was delighted for him, and we had a good number of Welsh players making the Test XV, with Byrney at 15, Jamie Roberts at 12, Stephen Jones at 10, Mike Phillips at 9 and AWJ at 4. I was joined on the bench by Bomb and Nugget. The South African side was very strong and their pack looked formidable with Tendai Mtawarira (or as more commonly known, The Beast), Bismarck du Plessis and John Smit in the front row. They had a second row of Bakkies Botha and Victor Matfield and a back row of Heinrich Brüssow, Juan Smith and Pierre Spies. Some genuine world-class talent there, and also in their backs, who included Fourie du Preez, Ruan Pienaar, Jean de Villiers and Bryan Habana. It was going to be a huge challenge but we couldn't wait.

The night before the first Test, I roomed with Donncha O'Callaghan, who had also been named on the bench. I was nervous the night before the game and the morning of the match, but I find being on the bench very different in terms of nerves to when you're starting a game. When you're a replacement you don't know if you'll be on at minute one or minute eighty. Often you're able to see better from that distance how the game's panning out, how the referee's allowing the game to play and then when you're called upon, can adapt your game accordingly. When you're on from the start, it's entirely different. You don't have that opportunity to reflect – you're caught up in the intensity of the game. It isn't until half-time when you're sitting down with the coaches that you're able to discuss how the game's going and the opportunities arising, and then you can go back out with those ideas in your head.

At half-time we were losing by 19 points to 7. We looked dangerous in attack and had scored a try through Tom Croft but we were struggling up front, especially in the scrum, where Phil Vickery in particular was having a torrid time against The Beast. The referee was on his case and he was being penalised often. Five minutes into the second half, Geech and the coaches made the decision to bring Phil off and replace him with Bomb. I kept looking at the clock every two minutes whilst sitting on the bench, hoping firstly I'd get on and secondly get a decent amount of game time. It had been a lifelong dream to play for the Lions, then suddenly I was being told to warm up, I was coming on. I was replacing Lee Mears, giving us an all-Welsh front row. There I was between two props I knew so well, representing the British and Irish Lions in front of millions of viewers – unreal. The first scrum we had went well and gave us and the other players' confidence. With less than 30 minutes to play we were down by 26 points to 7, but then Tom Croft scored another try, followed by another from Mike

Phillips. We had a number of opportunities but just couldn't quite get the tries and eventually ended up losing by 26 points to 21. We were absolutely gutted – we'd come back so well but South Africa had just held on. However, we had two more Tests to turn it around, and we still believed we could do that and win the series.

The week building up to the second Test was intense. We knew they'd target the scrums again and we had many scrum sessions, with Graham Rowntree working us as hard as possible. This may sound a bit big-headed but come the team announcement, I was certain I'd be selected after how the scrums had gone in the first half in the first Test, and how that had changed after I'd come on in the second half. Fortunately I was right: I was picked to start alongside Melon and Bomb in the first all-Welsh front row to start a British and Irish Lions Test since 1955 – a huge honour and achievement for all three of us. Simon Shaw was also brought into the side, replacing AWJ with his additional size and bulk in the front five. Shawsey's one of the biggest men I've ever seen on a rugby field, and he was brought in to do a job on South Africa's driving line-out – a weapon they loved to use. In the build-up to the second Test I roomed with Phil Vickery, and it's fair to say that after how the first Test had gone for him personally, he was very down. He had a few friends over for the tour and he had a few nights out to try and take his mind off what had happened. Phil's a great bloke and to see him down wasn't easy, but I was sure if given the chance, he'd bounce back.

That second Test in Pretoria is undoubtedly the hardest, most intense game of rugby I have ever played in. It was brutal at times, with huge hits going in from both sides and some incidents pushing the boundaries of what should be allowed on a rugby field. I think at the end of the game, seven or eight players had to visit hospital, including Melon and Bomb. Bomb suffered a dislocated shoulder after a shoulder charge from Bakkies Botha. Poor Melon suffered a fractured cheekbone as well, which didn't help his good looks – as I said, it was brutal and one hell of a game. We led 16 points to 8 at half-time after a try from Rob Kearney and a few successful kicks from Stephen Jones, but in the final quarter South Africa came roaring back with tries from Bryan Habana and Jacque Fourie. With a minute left, the scoreline was tied at 22 points all, when Ronan O'Gara (who was on as a replacement), secured a high kick. Rog made the decision to put in an up-and-under but as he got close to Fourie du Preez, who'd gone airborne to secure the kick, Rog stumbled and took du Preez out in the air. The referee blew for the penalty, and we were all in shock. Morné Steyn stepped up and from distance kicked the ball between the posts, giving South Africa the victory and the series. I remember going into the dressing room afterwards and we all sat in silence. I was numb – I'd played all 80 minutes and I just had nothing left. Poor Rog was in a right state after what had happened, being penalised for a stumble and taking out the player in the air. Those players who weren't going to hospital were all sitting in that dressing room stunned: we could so easily have been going into the third Test level, but now we had one Test to play to gain a victory against South Africa. Being whitewashed 3-0 in the series was something not worth thinking about. We had to win the following weekend.

A few days after the second Test match, we had the chance to go on a safari, which was a great opportunity and an experience you don't get too often. Two coaches were laid on, one for the players and the other for coaches and the backroom team. On the coaches there were some trays of beer for us to enjoy and quickly we started to have a few cans. The journey to our destination was going to take a few hours so we had plenty of time to have a few drinks. Around two and a half hours into the journey, a decision was made by management that people could still carry on to the safari destination, or if preferred you could return to Pretoria, where we were staying, and have a day on the beer. The Welsh, Irish and London Wasps boys all decided for that day we were going back to Pretoria – the safari could wait for another time. After that second Test we just wanted to chill out with a few laughs and drinks, to try to take our minds off rugby for a few hours.

In the training for the third Test, as always, there was no letting up. A number of players were either unavailable or carrying injuries, so the coaches had to see which of the walking wounded could make it for that final Test. Again I got the nod at hooker and this time, due to injuries, I'd be in the middle of a front row with Andrew Sheridan and Phil Vickery. Phil was desperate to put a few wrongs right and was fired up. We did make a few changes, what with injuries and just trying to freshen things up, so players such as Shane Williams, Riki Flutey, Joe Worsley and Nugget all got starts. In the build-up to the game we went through our usual video analysis, focusing particularly on one of the scrums in the second Test, where we managed to shove South Africa off their own ball, something that doesn't happen very often in international rugby and especially not with South Africa. Graham Rowntree was so happy with that clip that he said to us after it ended, "That's better than sex, that is, boys!" High praise indeed!

Prior to the third Test I roomed with Rob Kearney. Rob had come into the Test team in the first Test due to an injury to Byrney, and had played superbly. Before the final game of the tour and his last game as Lions coach, Geech gave a hugely emotional speech, which was made famous by the DVD that went with the tour. I have to say, I have huge admiration for the man.

The third Test was played in Johannesburg and as per the two other Tests, it was a superb game of rugby. We played some great stuff and scored some brilliant tries – Shane Williams got a brace and Ugo Monye scored an interception try – and Stephen Jones made five out of seven kicks count on the day. The forward pack went really well and Phil Vickery was able to exorcise some demons with a strong performance in the scrum up against a man he'd struggled with only a fortnight earlier, The Beast. I unfortunately had to come off just prior to half-time with concussion, to be replaced by Ross Ford, who gained his first Lions cap. Phil came off just before the hour mark to a rapturous reception from players and fans alike. Phil's a hugely likeable character, and a top player. In the first Test he just had one of those days, but he bounced back brilliantly in that third Test. One of my overriding memories from the tour is of him saying to me after the third Test that he wished I'd been next to him in the first Test, as he believed the scrum contest would have been completely different. To get that type of praise from a World Cup winner meant a lot to me, and it's something I'll never forget. After the win in the third Test, it's fair to say we had a good night mingling with all those amazing British and Irish Lions fans who'd spent thousands to be there with us to give us their support. I was so thankful they had a Test win to celebrate. We spent the following day on the beer as well, to say farewell to each other after a fabulous tour.

Ultimately we did lose the series on that South African tour, but the result could have been so different. As is the way when two outstanding sides clash, small margins make all the difference. We played ten games on the tour, winning seven, drawing one and losing just two, which were two of the Tests. I played in eight of those games, which I'm very proud of. I played alongside some outstanding players and we pushed the World Champions really close in their own backyard. It was one of my proudest achievements in my rugby career to represent the British and Irish Lions, and to play in the Tests in particular is something I'll always remember very fondly. Being a tourist's great but if I hadn't played in a Test, I'd always have looked back with a tinge of regret. Just look at Simon Shaw on that tour. Shawsey had toured to South Africa in 1997 but not appeared in a Test, then to New Zealand in 2005, again not playing in a Test. Then South Africa second time around with us, there he was at the age of 34 finally playing in a Test and putting in one of the greatest performances by an individual in a British and Irish Lions shirt on that day. His interview afterwards with Sky Sports summed up how he felt about being a Lions Test player – a special moment from a great guy.

We flew back to Britain on the Monday after the final Test and I was met at Heathrow Airport by my Uncle Dave and Becky to take me home in the car. On the way back, I asked why we were going a different route to normal through the lanes around Tonyrefail and they said that there were roadworks so there was no alternative. As we turned into Tonyrefail, the real reason for the detour became clear: the village primary school had a load of children out with banners welcoming me back, so we stopped to thank them and chat for a while. Setting off again, as we got close to Tonyrefail Rugby Club there were plenty of faces I recognised again with banners and wishing to thank me for my efforts. I have to say it was pretty special and made you realise how much being a Lion means to people. I'd missed my family as I'd been away for six weeks so it was great to see Becky and Brooke in particular, but I wouldn't have missed being a British and Irish Lion – there's such a heritage and tradition connected to it, and I'm still overwhelmed to this day about getting to be a part of it.

CHAPTER 12

From a Tulip to a Hammer

AFTER NINE YEARS at the Scarlets, in summer 2013 I was off on a new challenge. This time my destination was my local region, the Cardiff Blues. In addition to cutting down on my travel, allowing me to spend more time with my family, joining Cardiff Blues also gave me the opportunity to work with Phil Davies again. Phil was a coach I enjoyed playing for, and when I was discussing with him the potential move to Cardiff Arms Park, I liked what I heard. They had an exciting young squad, but had lost a few senior players in the last few years and were now looking to turn that around by bringing in some experience. Shortly after it was announced I was joining, it was also announced that my old mate Melon was coming back to Cardiff Blues after a spell out in France with Toulon. Melon hadn't really enjoyed the French scene, and was now returning to the capital city of Wales, and I couldn't wait to play alongside him again at regional level – something I hadn't done since the Celtic Warriors.

Another reason for my move was the facilities that Cardiff Blues have at the Vale of Glamorgan. The training area, the areas to relax in before and after training and the food that you're provided with are all top class, and the kit man, Mike Barriere, who's been there for a number of years, has your kits and everything else you need ready. It may sound a bit pampered, but having everything ready for you does make a difference to a player and makes the whole environment feel very professional. Very soon after I arrived, Phil Davies approached me to ask me to be captain. I was very honoured but did push back initially, as I felt there were a number of players who'd been at the region far longer than me who I felt could step up into a leadership role. However, Phil was very persuasive and made it clear that with my experience of captaining Scarlets and Wales and having been brought into the region as a senior player, I was the right man for the job. He therefore eventually succeeded in persuading me to take on the role of captain at the Cardiff Blues.

As mentioned earlier, there was a lot of exciting potential in the squad with young players such as Rhys Patchell, Harry Robinson, Owen Williams, Cory Allen, Kristian Dacey and Ellis Jenkins coming through. If I had to pick one young player who immediately caught my eye as a talent, then it would be Rhys Patchell. Patch is always very professional, prepares well for games and is constantly looking to improve – a fine rugby player. As we also had some already-established players such as Leigh Halfpenny, Alex Cuthbert, Melon, Gavin Evans, Taufa'ao Filise, Bradley Davies, Josh Navidi and Sam Warburton in our ranks, I was looking forward to the new season ahead playing for a new team. In pre-season that year, I felt in great condition – as good as I'd felt in a long time. A number of niggles had gone away and my fitness test results were as good as I had attained for many years. I was happy with my decision to move to Cardiff Blues and everything was going well in my rugby life and personally, so I felt I had a really good life balance.

My first appearance for the Cardiff Blues was away against Worcester Warriors. And as you often find with early pre-season games, we had one set of fifteen players starting the first half and then a completely new fifteen playing the second half. I played the first half and was happy with how my debut went, and we came out on top in the game, with a win. The following week we played at Cardiff Arms Park against Sale Sharks, with Peely in opposition, and again gained the victory.

We were playing some good rugby and things were looking very promising.

The first league game was away to Glasgow Warriors and we put up a decent display, with Patch scoring all our points through four penalties and a drop goal, but it wasn't enough and we went down to a defeat. We did win our first home league game to Connacht, but then suffered a very disappointing home loss to Zebre. It was a mixed bag of results in the League going into the Heineken Cup. The group we were drawn in was going to be tough, with Melon's old team Toulon, Exeter Chiefs and Glasgow Warriors. Our first game was away at Sandy Park against Exeter and we went into the game really fancying our chances, even though our form was a bit mixed at the time. Unfortunately Exeter played some really good stuff and caught us cold early in the first half, which gave them confidence and destroyed ours. Our defence in that first half was non-existent and by half-time they'd scored five tries, and had a bonus point within 30 minutes of the game starting. All in all, pretty mortifying, and when we trudged off at half-time, I felt so sorry for the fans that had travelled to cheer us on. It's safe to say Phil and Dale McIntosh were enraged with that performance, and basically told us to go out and stop embarrassing ourselves. We did score four tries in the second half to get some level of respectability back, but the damage had already been done and Exeter ran out 44 points to 25 winners. The following week we had Toulon coming to Cardiff, so a huge challenge awaited.

In the week building up to the Toulon game, the coaches changed the format of our working week. On the Monday we had a video debrief of the Exeter game, which at times was like a video nasty. We did weights on the Tuesday and on the Wednesday we went white-water rafting, to try to bring a bit of fun and team camaraderie in after the hammering the week before. Training returned to normal on the Thursday and the Friday, and I was looking forward to facing the French giants. Unfortunately, on the morning of the fixture I had to make the decision to pull out of the game after receiving some medical news which meant an enforced absence. On the pitch, what followed was a fantastic team performance to a man and a totally unexpected victory over Toulon, who had players in their line-up such as Matt Giteau, Jonny Wilkinson and Bakkies Botha, just to name a few. Gareth Davies scored the winning try and became a rugby hero to Cardiff Blues fans forever. The players and coaches were ecstatic, and rightly so. Toulon would go on to win the Heineken Cup that season, and the only team who defeated them in Europe all year was Cardiff Blues, which gives you some understanding of the achievement that day.

After beating Toulon, our European campaign carried on with a home game against Glasgow Warriors, which we won, though we then lost narrowly to them in Glasgow the following weekend. At this point a number of players were either out injured or were carrying injuries and the strength of our squad was being put under serious strain, The following week we played Toulon away and were taken apart – their forward power in particular was all too much for the boys. We conceded three penalty tries and also received four yellow cards on the day, such was the pressure we were under, and all of that was after we took an early lead through a try from our Samoan second rower, Filo Paulo!

After that loss the season really took a turn for the worse, with us losing our final group game at home to Exeter and suffering some poor results in the league. The final straw for Phil was at the start of March when we lost away to Zebre. There were a few contentious decisions during that match, but regardless of that, we did suffer a defeat to a team we shouldn't have been losing to at all, let alone them beating us both home and away that season. Two days after losing to Zebre, Phil made the decision to resign from his position as Director of Rugby at Cardiff Blues.

I wasn't surprised by the decision but I was still disappointed to see him go. Phil had brought some good young players through and his organisational skills are outstanding. However, although he was officially Director of Rugby, he was also doing a lot of the coaching, and I felt that if he had been left to perform his official role with a strong coach alongside him then who knows, things could have been a bit different. The biggest challenge as I saw it, though, was that whereas in previous years Cardiff Blues had a squad of players such as Ben Blair, Xavier Rush, Paul Tito, Casey Laulala and Jamie Roberts, all those players had now either retired or moved on and the finances were simply not in place to replace them with players of the same calibre. We had to look to players closer to home, try to bring young players through and try untested players at that level such as Chris Dicomidis, Geraint Walsh and Adam Thomas. A strategy like this is a risk if people are expecting instant results. With Phil leaving, Dale McIntosh and Paul John were put in charge. Both The Chief and Johnsey already got on well with the players and had our respect from what they'd achieved on the pitch themselves. The training changed, with shorter, sharper, more intense sessions and as the season was coming to an end, our performances did pick up. With us looking to play a more expansive game, decent weather definitely aids that brand of rugby and there were plenty of smiles on faces – winning certainly helps. I was pleased to make my comeback in late March in a win against Ulster at home and we then managed victories against Edinburgh away, Scarlets at Judgement Day and Connacht away before losing in the final league game to Scarlets at Parc Y Scarlets. We ended the season in seventh place in the league and did wonder after the upturn in results whether The Chief and Johnsey would be kept on. What we didn't know at that point was that the board were looking to bring in a high-profile coach to lift Cardiff Blues to new heights, and what a journey I and the Cardiff Blues were about to go on.

Mark Hammett was announced as Director of Rugby in May 2014. Hammer (as he was known in rugby circles) had been successful as a player, playing for the Crusaders and New Zealand as a hooker and winning many trophies. After retiring from playing, he'd become Assistant Coach at the Crusaders and then took over as Coach at the Hurricanes, known for their attacking brand of rugby. It seemed like a great piece of recruitment and that he'd be a coach who could really lead us in the right direction long term. The first time I met him was when I went to the Hilton Hotel in Cardiff with Richard Holland, the Chief Executive at Cardiff Blues, who had arranged a meeting with him and Gats. He proceeded to talk to us about his own ethos regarding the game, his plans for the Cardiff Blues and how he wanted us to play. It all sounded very impressive and I left there thinking we had a coach very similar in style to Gats, a coach I highly respect. Exciting times lay ahead for me and all Cardiff Blues players and followers, or so I thought.

With Hammett as Director of Rugby, the decision was made to keep The Chief and Johnsey on as coaches, which I felt they deserved. A new face amongst the front-line coaching staff was another New Zealander coming on board as Strength and Conditioning Coach, Paul Downes – someone that Hammett knew well from his Hurricanes days. Hammett had to return to New Zealand to tie up a few loose ends with the Hurricanes, but as pre-season was due to start shortly, The Chief and Johnsey took the sessions with support from Downesey. We'd made a few new signings, with Gareth Anscombe, Manoa Vosawai and Jarrad Hoeata coming on board, as well as a few others including my Wales and Lions colleague Adam Jones. Myself, Melon and Bomb could line up alongside each other again, this time for the Cardiff Blues. I liked the look of our recruitment and even though we'd lost Robin Copeland and Leigh Halfpenny – two fine players – and a few others, with what looked like a good new man at the helm, I went into the new season with optimism.

The fitness side of the training with Downesey involved a lot of running for long distances, much more than we'd experienced previously, but the players were happy to do it. With a new coaching group there are always changes, but the boys were keen to impress and competition in the squad was really good. We all wanted to play our part in making a fresh

140

start and build to being serious competitors in the League and Europe with Hammett at the helm.

Before the 2014–15 season started, Cardiff Blues went to Singapore to play in the inaugural World Club 10s tournament. Tragically Owen Williams was badly injured, severely damaging his spine, to this day making movement very difficult for him. Initially there were real concerns about total paralysis, but fortunately he's made great progress and is able to get about with the aid of crutches. Owen's a great boy with a brilliant attitude and family around him and how he dealt with his injury has been inspiring. He was a real talent, a great outside break as a centre and good in defence. He was already a Welsh international at the time of his injury aged only 22, and I have no doubt that he'd have gone on to win over 50 caps for his country with his rugby ability. What happened to him made you realise how precarious a rugby career could be, and reminded you we all should enjoy it while we can. His injury was a huge shock to all at the Cardiff Blues, to the rugby fraternity in general and in particular to his close pals such as Macauley Cook, who visited him daily during his time in hospital.

After a while, Hammett returned to our shores to take up his role as Director of Rugby and a few days later asked to have a face-to-face meeting with me. As I was captain, I didn't see anything unusual in this – captains often meet up with the Head Coach or Director of Rugby, depending on the club's set up. However, what transpired was one of the strangest meetings I've ever had in a rugby capacity, and really set the tone for what was coming with our new man in charge.

After the initial pleasantries had been exchanged, Hammett asked me bluntly "How close are you to Gethin Jenkins – are you mates?" I replied by saying I'd known Melon since junior rugby and we were good friends. What he said next, I couldn't believe – he asked me if I felt that Melon needed to change as a character. I was stunned: a man who'd been on three Lions tours, played for his country for many years and captained them many times, and was so highly thought of by his peers, and I was being asked if he needed to change. Sure, Melon can be miserable at times, but we all just let him get on with it. The man's a perfectionist and is always striving to be the best – he's a winner. I told Hammett that in my view he didn't need to change. It was obvious to me that Downesey had been relaying what he thought of certain players and coaches back to Hammett when he was in New Zealand, and clearly Melon was one he'd earmarked as a potential problem.

Once I told Hammett that I thought Melon didn't need to change, the way he responded showed that potentially we could be in for a power struggle and he was showing me who was boss. He said, "Bear in mind, I got rid of Andrew Hore and Ma'a Nonu from the Hurricanes." The message I took from that was that it was going to be his way and no compromises, no matter what your status in the game. I've always said that if Hammett had been in Cardiff for a few months and seen with his own eyes an issue with training, or people around the place not being professional or dragging others down, then that's one thing. But to take action like that based on information from a third party, his Strength and Conditioning Coach, about a player held in such high esteem is crazy. Hammett should have been interacting with influential senior players, explaining what he wanted and building up a leadership group to aid him, not alienating them.

We started the League season off by gaining some revenge against Zebre, with Patch scoring 21 points, but then the following week we lost heavily to Glasgow Warriors, where Fijian Niko Matawalu was in fine form, scoring a brace of tries. Losses against Ulster and Leinster followed, before drawing to Connacht. We then went on another poor run of games before gaining a victory in November against Benetton Treviso at home, in which our recent signing, Argentinian full back Joaquín Tuculet, showed what a fine player we'd acquired on a short-term deal. Alongside his fellow countryman and recent signing Lucas Amorosino, there were some glimpses of real attacking ability out wide if we could secure enough front-foot ball.

Due to our League position from the previous year, we missed out on the newly renamed European Rugby Champions Cup and instead played in the second tier competition, the European Rugby Challenge Cup. We were in a pool with London Irish, Grenoble and Rovigo Delta, and we got out of the pool in second place only then to lose in the knock-out stages in the next round to – of all teams – Newport Gwent Dragons, our local rivals down the road! Not ideal at all.

Off the field, training was intense. Hammett wanted the players to be in for training for longer each day. Previously we'd had the same type of intense sessions but over a shorter period. This new routine meant us hanging around waiting for the next session to occur. When we quizzed him as to why we were doing the sessions like this and raised the fact that there were times when we were waiting around, Hammett asked Downesey to arrange for mattresses to be brought in so that the players could have a rest and a sleep between sessions, if they liked. Luckily, common sense prevailed and this idea was abandoned. It felt to me and others that Hammett just didn't understand or appreciate the length of our rugby season in comparison to what he was used to in Super Rugby back in New Zealand, but when The Chief and Johnesy voiced their views on the training, it fell on deaf ears.

As mentioned earlier, we had a mixed set of results, especially before Christmas, and in addition to the training arrangements, the players weren't happy with certain things that were going on off the field. One such incident involved hooker Marc Breeze. Breezey was a really popular figure at the club, very well liked, but unfortunately for him, he'd picked up a number of injuries and during that season and the preceding one had rarely been seen on a rugby field. With his contract due to expire that coming summer, he was desperate to prove his worth to the squad, as Hammett had never had the opportunity to see him play. Breezey's wife had just had their first child and he was regaining fitness when Hammett advised him that he could leave straight away if he wanted to find a new club.

Breezey was devastated: we were in October and where could he move to at that point? He did stay till the end of the season but he and all of us knew that his time was up. The players weren't happy with such treatment of a popular teammate, who in a stretched squad wasn't given an opportunity to show his worth.

In October we also lost heavily to the Ospreys in the League. As captain, the players asked me to speak to Hammett, as they felt things weren't working out and they wanted it addressed and worked through. Melon and I did have a meeting with Hammett but when we advised him that the players were not happy, his initial response was that if players were not happy, they could leave. I remember asking him, "What, all the players can leave?" The meeting did go on to look at the working week and some of the other player issues – changes were made to bring the working week back to what the players had been used to before Hammett took charge, but in general it was clear that in his view, with the game preparation we were doing, things would work out eventually.

Also that month it was announced that Rhys Williams, a young hooker at the region, was to be offered a new contract. I was really surprised at this as Rhys had hardly played all season – I would be out of contract at the end of the season and in my view this was further evidence that Hammett wanted me out, with Rhys taking up one of the available hooker slots. I asked my agent to start looking elsewhere. I did speak to Peter Thomas, who said that the contracts were down to Hammett. If he remained, then as far as I could see, I wasn't going to be at the Cardiff Blues – be it his decision or my own.

Whilst training one day in November, we found out about a story that Hammett had done with Wales Online where he stated that Welsh rugby was 15 years behind New Zealand. As you can imagine, seeing that the group weren't too happy with the way the season was going with him as it was, reading that did nothing to improve their mood or opinion. With Hammett you just didn't know what he was thinking, and it seemed that he was always wanting to make a statement of intent to us. As mentioned earlier, it seemed that he and the players were locked in a power struggle, and I have no idea why he behaved like that. I can only speak for myself, but for me it got to the point where when I came into training and saw his car was there, I felt like turning my car around and going home. It got so bad that I was considering retiring from the game and walking away – that's how low I was feeling about the whole thing.

Amongst the playing group and coaches, we had a fining system where if you missed a meeting, were late or committed one of a number of other misdemeanours then you had to pay a fine. If the fine wasn't paid, it increased each week until it was, and at the end of the season all money from fines was put towards an end-of-season event. I was put in charge of this, and following the injury suffered by Owen Williams, we decided to donate 50% of the money raised every season to him and his fabulous charity, Stay Strong For Ows, which we love to support. This fining system was a bit of fun and we all bought into it. Well, when I say 'all', that's not quite true.

During this particular season, Downesey accidently flooded the dressing room with water, so I put his name up on the board that we had for fines. His name was still on there as unpaid when Hammett took me to one side. He asked for Downesey's name to be removed from the board and said that he didn't agree with having a fine system and that he was stopping it. The players weren't happy and asked me to approach the then Cardiff Blues Chairman, Peter Thomas. I explained to Peter what had happened, and he said that if the players wanted it reinstated then we should reinstate it. So we did, much to Hammett's annoyance – mind you, I don't recall if Downesey ever paid his fine or not.

Back to the playing field, and as stated earlier, it was a disappointing season with a number of losses. We did earn a good win at home to the Scarlets in February, but bar a few wins in the pool stages in Europe, it was a poor season. We lost three times to the Newport Gwent Dragons that year, which to Cardiff Blues fans is almost unforgiveable. Come the end of February, we were away to Benetton Treviso, and suffered a heavy loss by 40 points to 24. The following day it was announced that Hammett would be leaving the Cardiff Blues for family reasons and returning to New Zealand. I think it's fair to say I wasn't too disappointed.

The strange thing is that in the week building up to the Benetton game, I had a long discussion with Hammett about rugby in general which, bar our first ever meeting in the Hilton Hotel, was the most positive conversation we had in six months. It was almost if it was just two rugby men talking, with no pressure of a boss and employee relationship, as he knew he would soon be leaving. It was all very odd. Hammett had left only six months into a three-year contract, and The Chief and Johnsey were again asked to take over the reins in a less-than ideal situation to take us through to the end of the season. After what had happened the last time they'd been put in temporary charge, they knew that was all it was going to be: temporary. We ended the League season in tenth place, ahead only of Benetton Treviso and Zebre – the region's worst ever final league position.

That season with Hammett was really difficult. As I said, I was on the verge of quitting rugby altogether until I thought about how hard I'd worked to get where I was, and that one man wouldn't push me away from rugby. All in all, it was a really tough year and Cardiff Blues were yet again in the market for a new Head Coach/Director of Rugby. I was out of contract and in all my years of playing professional rugby, this was the one year I felt like retiring. Luckily, the season really changed from when Hammett was in charge to when The Chief and Johnsey took over again, as had been the case when they'd taken over the previous year.

CHAPTER 13

The Only Way Is Up

As MENTIONED IN the previous chapter, my contract with Cardiff Blues was due to expire at the end of the 2014–15 season. With Hammett moving on, I kept open discussions with Peter Thomas, who told me in a phone conversation that they wanted to keep me but that ultimately it was down to the Head Coach. My agent was also having regular discussions with the CEO, Richard Holland. In mid-March I was told a contract would be sent to my agent but then at the end of March I was informed that no new contract would be offered due to lack of funds available to sign me. This came as a real blow to me. I missed the end of that season with an injury to my shoulder which needed surgery, so I was now close to the summer break with no club for the following season.

It was around this time that The Chief announced he was off to Merthyr RFC as forwards coach. Shortly after The Chief had taken up his new position, Lee Jarvis, who was Head Coach at Merthyr, contacted me to say that Stan Thomas (chairman of Merthyr and brother of Cardiff Blues Chairman Peter) had heard that I might be available and wanted to know if I'd be interested in joining them. Merthyr had some big plans and wanted me to be a part of them. I had a meeting with Lee and Stan Thomas in a restaurant in Cardiff, where they offered a lucrative contract which increased in value as the meeting went on, showing how keen they were to get me on board. The

Chief did speak to me directly about joining and I said that I'd have a think about it, but I really felt I had another year in me at a higher level – no disrespect to Merthyr. My agent set up a meeting with the Worcester Warriors about potentially joining them. Dean Ryan was their Director of Rugby and I travelled to Worcester and met him at the Sixways Stadium, and had a really positive conversation. I liked what he had to say and I did start thinking that this might be the best move for me at that stage in my career. In May 2015, it was announced by BBC Sport that I was leaving the Cardiff Blues, though I actually still hoped there was time to turn that decision around and remain a Cardiff Blues player.

Worcester offered a very attractive playing contract. They'd gained promotion to the Aviva Premiership, and even though Dean made it clear I wasn't going to be first-choice hooker initially, I saw pitting myself against teams from that League as a challenge I'd savour. However, in June, it was announced that Danny Wilson was going to become Head Coach at Cardiff Blues. I knew Danny well from his time coaching at the Scarlets and from his work with Wales so contacted him to congratulate him, and during the conversation I told him my situation at Cardiff Blues. Danny wanted me to stay as he wanted a strong front five as the base to play off, and wanted me to be part of that. I told him that I'd be interested in staying but that there currently didn't appear to be a place for me in the playing squad. Danny said he'd see what he could do.

It got to the point where Worcester required an answer to their contract offer. All it needed was my signature. My agent had been negotiating with them and he was keen for me to get the deal done in time for pre-season. Whilst I was mulling it over, Danny contacted me to let me know that there was a contract offer from Cardiff Blues and to ask if I'd sign. The contract discussions were completed entirely between me and Danny – I didn't want my agent involved. I wanted to do it on my own as the initial negotiation for a contract extension with Cardiff Blues had been conducted by my agent with no contract materialising. Secondly, Danny had had to juggle a few things around to enable them to make the offer, which was final, with no room to manoeuvre on finances, so it didn't make sense to pay anyone a percentage for negotiating a deal when there was nothing to negotiate.

The contract with Cardiff Blues offered less money than the Worcester one and was also only for one year, rather than the two years offered by Worcester, so there was a lot to consider for me. However, having thought it over long and hard, I made the decision to stay on at the Cardiff Blues. Danny was a coach I believed would be good to work under after my experiences with him, and I looked forward to him making us a better side. Also, there'd no need to move house or make long commutes, and I could complete my rehabilitation after my shoulder operation with the Cardiff Blues physios, who I knew well. I informed Worcester that I wouldn't be signing the contract, which they accepted, but my agent wasn't impressed at all by my decision. However, ultimately it was my decision.

The Cardiff Blues position would be Danny's first role as Head Coach at a senior level. He'd coached at London Welsh, Newport Gwent Dragons, Wales U20s, Scarlets and Bristol, all mainly as a forwards coach, but now was moving up to be the top man in the coaching structure. I liked what I'd seen from him and was keen to see how he would do in this position. With a forwards coaching background, he instantly put a lot of emphasis on the set piece. He was keen to strengthen the forwards pack with size and power, which you can see from his recruitments over his stint as coach with the Cardiff Blues, such as front five players Anton Peikrishvili, Salesi Ma'afu, Rhys Gill, Kirby Myhill and George Earle – with some of those recruits working out better than others!

In terms of Danny's coaching style, he's a very detailed coach who puts a lot of responsibility on players to know their roles and to do their own homework on the opposition on top of the support on analysis from the coaches. The players go out with a game plan from him, but he does encourage players to express themselves. Alongside Danny were Paul John as assistant coach and Graham Steadman as defensive coach. Graham had made his name in Rugby League (as many Rugby Union defence coaches do), but had also coached at Sale and Newcastle, plus as a defensive coach with Scotland and Ireland. Danny wanted an experienced defensive coach on board as we really needed to step up in defence – he had real focus on us gaining respect again as a region and put a lot of onus on us to get wins and be competitive against the other Welsh regions.

Our first League game of the season was at home to Zebre and we ran out 61 points to 13 winners, a very pleasing scoreline to start the season with. Due to the Rugby World Cup being played in September, we lost a number of players, as did the other sides in the Pro12. As Cardiff was a venue for the World Cup, with Cardiff Arms Park being used as fanzone where rugby fans could meet to watch matches, the next few games were played away. We lost all four games against Leinster, Connacht, Munster and Ulster but stayed in each of those games, not losing any game by more than nine points and picking up bonus point losses to Ulster and Connacht due to finishing within seven points. As I mentioned, we were missing players on World Cup duty, but where games started to move away from us was when it came time to bring on replacements when players tired. The Irish Provinces just had more depth than us within their squads, the game against Leinster in particular illustrating this. We were still in the game after 60 minutes, but when both benches were used as the starting XVs tired in the last 20 minutes, they ran away from us.

In terms of the Welsh derbies, we beat Newport Gwent Dragons home and away, with the away win courtesy of a late penalty from Patch to gain the victory by one point. Scarlets we also beat home and away, with the win at Parc-y-Scarlets in April perhaps the best performance of the season. Ospreys beat us twice in the League including a big win on Judgement Day at the Millennium Stadium, where they were just too strong for us. There were some good performances that season in addition to the games already mentioned, such as beating Munster and Ulster at home. That season with Patch and Gareth Anscombe playing 15 and 10 respectively for us, it worked so well. With two excellent distributors on the pitch who could also break through a gap, we scored some excellent tries.

In terms of Europe, we beat Calvisano home and away comfortably, but lost home and away to Harlequins. In the home game, I was sent off for the first time in my professional career for a stamp on England international Nick Easter. I received a seven-week ban for the incident, reduced from the initial eleven-week ban due to my previous disciplinary record. Though I really regretted the momentary lapse from my usual standards, the seven-week ban did mean I had Christmas off, so it wasn't the worst timing for picking one up.

We did beat Montpellier convincingly at home and lost by only one point to them away, with them scoring a last-minute try which was converted to get the win. After we'd been in front, losing like that was really tough for the boys to take. In terms of my season, I had a slow start due to the shoulder operation, but I slowly got more game time and as the season went on, I was in a good battle with Kristian Dacey for the starting hooker spot. When I started the season, I thought it would be my last, but as the season went on, I was in good form and my body felt good. In April, Cardiff Blues brought in Kirby Myhill from the Scarlets – another hooker. I had a chat with Danny, who was happy with my performances, and after speaking to Peter Thomas, another contract was offered to me, which I was very happy to sign for the following season.

During the summer before the 2016–17 season, Cardiff Blues brought in Matt Sherratt as backs and attack coach. Jockey (as he's known) had worked with Danny previously at Bristol RFC, so they knew each other well. The players warmed to Jockey almost instantly because of his enthusiasm and his intent to attack with real purpose. He concentrated a lot on ball skills with the players and made training fun and interesting. That pre-season we did something a bit different, with the players coming in for two weeks of training at a time and then having a week off, which kept us fresh. We'd made some good signings with Matthew Morgan, George Earle, Nick Williams and Willis Halaholo coming in; though we were unfortunately losing Patch to the Scarlets. Given my experience there, he'd had a chat with me about a possible move to the region and I told him it was a great place to play and would be a good step for him – their brand of rugby and the fact that Stephen Jones was the backs coach there would aid Patch in developing his all-round game. He wanted to play at 10 on a regular basis and his way was being blocked at Cardiff Blues by Gareth Anscombe. It was a real shame for us that he left as the pair playing together had been creating real opportunities out wide in attack, and with Jockey now on board and the way he wanted to play, with his focus on attack, who knows how much danger they could have caused for opposing defences?

We started the League season really well, including wins at home to Edinburgh and Glasgow and away victories at Munster and Zebre, playing some great rugby in those games. At the beginning of October, we suffered our first League loss at home to Leinster. We led by ten points at half-time but Jonny Sexton put in a great performance in the second half to gain the win by three points. The following week we went to Ospreys and were soundly beaten – we were really taken apart up front in a very disappointing performance. After a really promising start to the League season, we suffered a number of defeats between then and Boxing Day, when we got a win over local rivals Newport Gwent Dragons.

If I'm honest, we didn't really hit form in the League again until March, when we lost by a single point away to Leinster, drew with Ulster (also away) and then into April got revenge on Ospreys for the game earlier in the season, and the previous Judgement Day. We soundly beat them at the Principality Stadium by 35 points to 17, where Chicken (as Gareth Anscombe's nicknamed) was outstanding. That victory over Ospreys was our first win in the League against them since 2010.

In Europe we had some success, beating Pau home and away with two really good performances. We also beat Bath at home and Bristol both home and away, which meant we'd qualified for the knock-out stages. This was great for the players, coaches and fans alike. In the quarter-final we faced Gloucester at their home ground, Kingsholm. We were well in the game until midway through the second half when they moved away and ended up convincing winners, eventually going on to lose to Stade Français in the final. As Stade won the final, they would play off against us for the final European Champions Cup spot, following a new format brought in where the winners of the Challenge Cup would play off against the team who finished the league season in the next available slot outside of automatic qualification.

We played them in Paris and did lead at half-time, but due to a number of injuries, fatigue and Stade really ramping up their performance in the second half, they won emphatically. They therefore claimed the final spot, meaning that for the third consecutive year we'd miss out on playing in the major European rugby competition. As a group, we still lacked depth in certain areas but we did feel we were moving in the right direction, and with a push on recruitment to blend in with the talent we already had on our books, we felt that the following season we could really push to get into the Champions Cup.

Going into Danny's third year in charge, I was again offered a new contract – quite a turnaround from supposedly leaving two years earlier. I felt in good shape and was happy with my surroundings, so was very pleased to sign. I was looking to broaden my skills and had spoken to Danny about getting some experience of coaching, with an eye on my future after retiring from playing. He found out about an opportunity at Pontypridd and after speaking to Justin Burnell, Head Coach at Ponty, I agreed to help out there once a week as scrum coach, a skill I've always enjoyed. I looked forward to working with Justin, an experienced coach. As the season went on, I got more involved with Ponty, ending up doing a few nights a week and also taking charge of set pieces, all with Danny's blessing. I've really relished working alongside Justin and I've learnt a lot from a coaching perspective. It's been brilliant to have the chance to coach at the club which gave me my breakthrough into top-flight rugby and my first professional contract.

In terms of recruitment, Danny and Cardiff Blues had already recruited Ulster second rower Franco van der Merwe, who was coming on board pre-season. I'd played against him a few times and he was really respected and a fan favourite at Ulster, so getting him was a major coup and gave us a real physical presence in the second row. However, during pre-season training, it was announced that van der Merwe was moving on, without playing a game for us. A decision had been made that due to finances, he'd be released. For Danny, this was a real blow. He'd been in discussions with the Cardiff Blues board for a while about the playing budget, and now that he'd managed to bring in a player of van der Merwe's quality and experience, that player was being moved on. It was not frustrating just for Danny but for us players too.

In pre-season we played a game in London against London Scottish. The whole playing squad, including those not playing in the match and the coaches, stayed two nights (paying for the second night's accommodation ourselves) and on the Saturday evening and the Sunday had quite a few drinks to allow the squad to come together after a hard pre-season. We all travelled back on the Monday, so had a short training week, not the normal build-up for the home game against Exeter Chiefs on the Friday. Luckily, we still beat them. Exeter were the reigning English Champions, and they had a decent side out on the day, which gave us real confidence.

Following on from van der Merwe's departure, we also lost Graham Steadman as defence coach. Graham was a good coach and well-liked by the players as a really good bloke, but where I felt he struggled was in trying to get his point across clearly to us on his defensive policies – players seemed unsure what he wanted at times. Replacing Graham on a part-time consultancy basis would be Shaun Edwards. Shaun continued in his Wales role but also usually came in for one day a week at Cardiff Blues and took us through defensive drills. The defence stepped up another level, as the season ahead showed, with Shaun and his coaching knowledge and intensity playing a massive part in that. Richard Hodges, who was aiding us on contact work in the tackle area, supported Shaun on defence, as Shaun was normally only with us one day a week and not always available on match days. Hodges did an excellent job, working hard on defence with the players and coming up with different drills, which the players enjoyed and bought into.

Our confidence from beating Exeter was soon knocked out of us when we lost our first League game at home to Edinburgh and then away to Leinster by 37 points to 9 – a big loss, but they scored three converted tries in last 15 minutes. Soon after, we lost at home by one point to Glasgow, so unlike the season before, where we'd got off to a good start, this was the complete opposite. We did, however, gain an away win at Connacht, never an easy place to get a victory. Days later, though, some news broke which came as a blow to us all: our coach Danny Wilson would be leaving at the end of the season.

As a coach, Danny has always been very honest with his players whenever possible. He had regular meetings with a leadership group of players which included me, where we discussed any challenges the players had on and off the field. Danny would also discuss with us upcoming training plans, any travel arrangements, etc., and his views on how things were progressing. We knew as a group that Danny was looking to take the club forward but was facing challenges with the board regarding player budgets – a number of players being out of contract at the end of the season, including me – and didn't feel they were on the same page, as evidenced by the van der Merwe incident. Given the uncertainty created by all of that, when the news broke that he was leaving, it wasn't a surprise to us, but that didn't make it any less disappointing.

The players got together and all said that if this was going to be our last season with this group, then we wanted to do all we could to make it special. The playing group and all staff were very tight, all pulling in the same direction – we'd made improvements each season under these coaches and now this group was coming to an end, which was a real shame. Danny didn't change his approach and his determination was as strong as if he'd been staying with us for another three years: he wanted us to succeed even if he was moving on. In December we also found out that Jockey would be leaving Cardiff Blues. This wasn't a surprise after Danny's decision, but I knew how big a loss both of them leaving would be. Both excellent coaches and both top blokes – I'd definitely say they're both among the best coaches I've ever worked with.

Through all this upheaval and uncertainty, in terms of what was going on the pitch I was really pleased with my own performances, and yet again started wondering if retiring at the end of the season was premature. I was being selected in a number of games ahead of Kristian Dacey, and Danny and the coaches were happy with how things were going. As early as October 2017 I spoke to Richard Holland about a new contract but Dickie, as he's known, advised that this decision would have to be made by the new head coach. My agent by this point had changed and is now someone who's a well-known figure at Cardiff Blues: ex-Welsh international and British Lion Bob Norster. Bob kept contacting Dickie about the possibility of a new contract, but the response was a consistent message of no decision until they knew who the head coach was and what he wanted. It was an interesting dynamic with Bob speaking to Dickie, as Bob had previously been CEO at Cardiff RFC and Cardiff Blues so knew about the finances and how the role worked, and therefore understood the pressures and the responsibilities Dickie had.

In the League we gained some good wins over the Dragons, Connacht, Munster, Ulster and Southern Kings, one of the new entrants into the expanded League of 14. We also suffered some losses – some narrow, including to the Cheetahs. After a horrendous journey to get there, we lost after eight minutes of injury time resulted in a penalty try given against us which gave them the win. In the win against Ulster, I picked up a knee injury – I went to make a tackle and in the process got caught awkwardly by Ellis Jenkins on the side of my knee. The physio did a series of tests and all seemed fine, so I asked him to strap it up so I could continue. Minutes later I threw into a line-out in a planned move where I was due to come around the corner and carry the ball away. However, as I came around the corner, my knee just gave way and I ended up on the floor, not even managing to receive the planned pass. As we had lost the ball, I got up and got myself into the defensive line, but again my knee just gave out under me. I knew something serious was up and I had to come off.

In the changing room after the game, Peter Thomas could see how down I was, as I knew in all likelihood my season was over, and he told me that they'd look after me, which lifted my spirits a bit. That evening I went out with Melon and had a few drinks. He was also awaiting a new contract that was dragging on, and Peter had told him in the dressing room that they'd look after him too – a week later Melon signed his new contract. The knee didn't feel right that evening, but by the time I woke up the following morning it had swollen up like a balloon. After having it examined, it turned out I'd torn my ACL and would be out for six to nine months. No time's a good time to get an injury, but at that point I'd still not been offered a new contract. Now with my season over, I worried that they wouldn't want to take a risk on a 37 year old having an ACL reconstruction, but I was hoping that Peter would be true to his word in the changing room and offer me that contract.

In Europe we were having a great journey. In our pool we beat Lyon home and away as well as Toulouse home and away – two really strong French sides. We lost to Sale away but beat them at home, meaning we'd qualified for the knockout stages for the second consecutive year. In the quarter-finals we were away to Edinburgh. It felt like Edinburgh underestimated us, as they were in a good run of form at the time, but from the Ulster game onwards we'd been in excellent form, scoring some great tries and were full of confidence. Tactically, we played a very clever game in poor conditions, kicking well behind their back three, who struggled with the conditions and the accuracy of our kicking game. Unlike the year before at this stage, the boys put in a strong performance for 80 minutes and came out on top, with our defence being absolutely outstanding. We'd play the top seeds, Pau, at home in the semi-finals. At Cardiff Arms Park we played well, but in the last 15 minutes we really soaked up the pressure and again our defence was excellent. The hard-working team ethic and desire to win in front of our fans, who'd supported us so well all season, was very evident. The boys didn't want to let them down, and we succeeded in that aim by getting the victory. A total of five wins against French sides in a cup run is some achievement. The final would be against Gloucester in Bilbao.

Thousands of Cardiff Blues fans made their way to Bilbao, by plane, boat, train and car, creating a fantastic atmosphere in the town. Unfortunately, I couldn't make the trip to Bilbao due to my injury and a pre-scheduled dinner that also included Sam Warburton. We were the only two Cardiff Blues players who didn't make it there. The game itself was fantastic. Gloucester lead at half-time by 20 points to 6, but a great try from Tomos Williams and a superb effort from Garyn Smith put us right back in the game. Gloucester then restored their lead with another try, only for Blaine Scully to score a late try – unfortunately, Chicken missed a difficult conversion to leave us still behind. However, in the last minute, he redeemed himself with a penalty opportunity which he nailed between the posts. The referee blew up and Cardiff Blues were the European Challenge Cup Champions! Winning that trophy was a great send-off for Danny and Jockey as well as Tongan prop Taufa'ao Filise, who was retiring at 40 years of age (allegedly – many think he's older!). He'd been a mainstay in the Cardiff Blues front row for 13 years and took on all tight-head props who came to the club during his time, and due to fitness and mostly down to Fa'ao being a great prop, he's come out on top. A quiet man but a great man, and I wish him and his family well on his retirement.

As the season was coming to an end, still no playing contract was being offered to me. The message kept coming back that it would be down to whoever the new coach was. As that search continued, with names such as Jim Mallinder and Geordan Murphy being linked but not coming to fruition, the waiting went on whilst I was recuperating from my knee operation. I spoke to Danny and Jockey and wished them both well and thanked them for their efforts – I and the players both staying and leaving were delighted that we were able to have a successful last season with them, winning a cup and qualifying for the Champions Cup under their leadership, as they deserved it. Danny, due to be joining London Wasps as forwards coach to work with Dai Young, was suddenly offered an opportunity as forwards coach with Scotland, which he couldn't turn down. Jockey's to be backs coach at Ospreys, and I fully expect both to be very successful in their roles – though especially in Jockey's case, not too successful, I hope!

Finally, Cardiff Blues announced who their new head coach was going to be: Australian John Mulvihill, who's had experience coaching in Australia and most recently Japan. A few weeks later, I had a chat over the phone with John where he talked about his plans and how he wanted to play, and it all sounded very encouraging. I mentioned my situation to him and he seemed surprised, as he'd been under the impression that I wanted to get into coaching with Cardiff Blues rather than continuing in a playing capacity. I explained that I've been involved in coaching with Pontypridd for one season, but that I still wanted to continue my playing career. John said to leave it with him and he'd see what he could do. A short while later, a meeting was arranged with Bob, Peter and me, and I did receive a playing contract with Cardiff Blues – a rolling one-year contract – as Peter was confident I'd return from my knee injury. I signed the contract to continue my career with the Cardiff Blues. At the point of writing this book I don't see myself being back playing until November/December, but when I'm back, I'll have been playing at the top level in Wales for 18 years, something I'm very proud of.

Overall I've had a fantastic career to date and I'm really looking forward to working with John Mulvihill, the new coaches and some of the new recruits that have already been signed, such as Dmitri Arhip, who'll hopefully be lining up alongside me in the front row in the League and in Champions Cup rugby this season. Let's see if I can still hold my own at the top level. I know one thing for sure: there certainly won't be any lack of effort on my part.

Chapter 14

Battling Cancer

THE STORY OF my battle with this awful disease begins back in April 2013. I noticed a lump on one of my testicles, but wasn't in any discomfort so didn't think too much about it. A few weeks later, I was selected to play for the Barbarians, a fantastic rugby side that players receive invitations to play for. It was my first ever time selected and it's a real honour to don the famous black and white hooped jersey worn by so many rugby greats. It was a two-match tour, with my first appearance for the team against England at Twickenham.

Named in the Barbarians touring squad alongside me were four other Welshmen: Paul James, Duncan Jones, Dwayne Peel and James Hook. After the England match, we went to Hong Kong to play the British and Irish Lions in preparation for their upcoming tour. Being part of a very rare game between these two world-renowned sides was a very special feeling. I'd been a Lion only four years earlier, so playing a small part in helping the new Lions side get ready for the upcoming Test series against Australia was a real privilege. Whilst in Hong Kong, as the lump hadn't changed, I made the decision that when I returned to Wales, I'd go and see the Wales team doctor.

The doctor completed an examination and told me that there was nothing to worry about. I received a course of antibiotics to take, and all expectations were that the lump would go away. The pre-season was my first with the Cardiff Blues, and as mentioned previously, I was feeling in really good shape. My fitness results were as good as if not better than they'd ever been. I was free of niggling injuries, not coming into pre-season off the back of an operation, and for the first time in a long time, I had a full pre-season to prepare for the upcoming rugby year. I'd also just been announced as the captain for the new season, so with all these good things going on, I didn't really think too much about the lump. At the end of August, though, I went to see Gareth Jones, the team doctor at Cardiff Blues, as the lump was still there. It hadn't changed in size from what I could see and feel, but I just wanted it checked as it had now been a while since I'd first spotted it in April, with no improvement. I explained to Gareth about my previous visit to the Wales doctor and he completed an examination – his conclusion was the same: nothing to worry about, and another course of antibiotics.

In October 2013, Cardiff Blues travelled to Exeter to play them in a Heineken Cup tie. The game was played on a Sunday afternoon, and in the morning when the boys were getting strapped for the game, I spoke to the team doctor again. I'd now finished two courses of antibiotics and the lump was still there, though I was still in no discomfort. The team doctor said that once we got back from Exeter, he'd refer me to a consultant. I captained the team that day – unfortunately to a loss – and was still not overly concerned about this lump that stubbornly wouldn't go away.

The appointment with the consultant took place early the following week, prior to the Toulon Heineken Cup game. The consultant was Richard Coulthard and I met him at the Spire Hospital in Cardiff. After a thorough examination, I was referred for a CT scan. During the consultation, Richard told me that he wasn't excluding any possibilities about what the lump was, but we needed to find out what it was. I was told that regardless of the scan's findings, I needed an operation to remove the testicle, in a procedure called an orchiectomy. At that point, even though it may seem hard to believe, I was still thinking more about Cardiff Blues and rugby. I spoke to Phil Davies – still Cardiff Blues Director of Rugby then – and said that I'd need an operation, but that I'd delay it until November, when the Autumn Internationals were on. I was sure I wouldn't be needed by Wales, and Cardiff Blues had a big Heineken Cup game against Toulon in October which I wanted to be part of. This plan of action was about to be turned upside down, as indeed were my and my family's lives.

Just to backtrack slightly, I'll explain the week running up to the news that changed my life. The build-up to the Toulon game was well underway and I was training as normal, looking forward to captaining the side against the star-studded French team. On the Monday we had a day off, on the Tuesday morning some weights and a review of the previous game, in the afternoon we went white-water rafting at Cardiff Bay and then I had the meeting with Richard Coulthard in which he advised me that the testicle would have to be removed. On the Wednesday I had a day off and on the Thursday had the meeting with Phil to let him know that I'd need the operation, but that I was willing to wait till November for it. I trained on Thursday as normal and on the Friday morning I did the captain's team run and then went to have the CT scan in the afternoon. At 5.30 p.m. on Friday 18th October 2013, Richard called to break the news that it had spread into a lymph node in my stomach and that he was pretty sure it was cancer. He said I needed a biopsy as soon as possible, from which we'd know for certain what it was.

The first thought I had in my head was, was I going to die? Then I thought about my family: how would they cope? And also my rugby career being over. I just couldn't believe it – cancer? I was too young, surely? Shortly after I took the call from Richard, Becky came home. I broke the news to her and we both broke down. What was going to happen during this process, we just didn't know.

I went to bed that night with a thousand thoughts going through my head, but at that point I still wanted to play the following day against Toulon. I thought that might be my last game, and playing at a packed Cardiff Arms Park one last time was how I wanted to go out. However, when I awoke the following morning and thought things over, I realised that mentally I was in no position to play. I spoke to John Miles, the physio at Cardiff Blues at the time, and broke the news to him. He was stunned and passed on his sympathies. As we know, Cardiff Blues were outstanding that day and got the win over Toulon – a fantastic day for the team and the fans. I was happy they won, but I think everyone will understand that I had other things than celebrating a victory on my mind at that point.

The following week I spent time with close family and friends, advising them of the situation. We didn't tell Brooke because she was only six at the time, and we didn't feel she needed to know, especially when we'd have to wait for test results to know for absolute sure. I had the operation to remove one of my testicles on 24th October and then had to wait two weeks for the biopsy results. It felt like two months waiting to find out what the outcome was.

Becky and I travelled to the Spire Hospital on 7th November to receive the news from Richard, really apprehensive about the outcome of the biopsy. We were told it was indeed testicular cancer, but that we'd caught the cancer early. Richard explained that there are two different types of testicular cancer, seminoma and nonseminoma, and I was diagnosed with seminoma cancer. Richard was trying to be as positive as possible, but in reality the only word I heard coming out of his mouth was 'cancer'. Treatment would start in a week's time, and I knew I had a battle on my hands, but I was determined to get through it.

After hearing the news, Becky and I stopped for a coffee at Cardiff Gate on the journey home to talk things through and put a plan in place re who we needed to tell immediately, like family and friends. Our first stop was at Becky's mum's to tell her the news and then I went to the Vale, Cardiff Blues' training facility, and told Phil that I had cancer. He was amazing with me. He said he knew I'd get through it and that they'd support me all the way, in whatever I needed. Gareth Jones and John Miles were also great and said if I needed to talk about anything, just to let them know. They said that they'd get the squad together and make them aware. I didn't want to be there for that meeting as it was all still too raw for me, so I left, but I appreciated all the support. I spent the next day or so letting family and close friends know that I had cancer, and shortly after that Cardiff Blues released a statement to the media informing them of my condition.

When I was given the news about it being cancer, I was told not to go on the internet to try to find out more as there is so much incorrect information online. Obviously I ignored this and immediately put 'testicular cancer' into the search engine, and they are right – there are some real horror stories being put out there.

I was advised by the doctors that prior to the chemotherapy, you could have a procedure to freeze your sperm if you potentially wanted the opportunity to extend your family in the future. After speaking to Becky, I was going to do this, but as it turned out the initial appointment was cancelled and the only time they could complete this procedure was the morning of the operation. I declined the offer after again speaking to Becky – we decided we were happy with the size of our family, plus having that procedure on the day of the operation was a bit too much for me to deal with.

I'd be undergoing chemotherapy to try to overcome this disease, and I'd be a patient at Velindre Hospital in Whitchurch, Cardiff. When I first got there, I couldn't believe what it was like in the waiting room waiting to be called; it was like a cattle market. There were all these people in one public area, waiting for their names to be called to be seen. I'd been expecting the process to be far more private – it wasn't what I'd expected at all. When I was called, I was taken into a room where what was going to happen was explained, blood tests were taken and the consultant gave me a leaflet about chemo and side effects such as hair loss. I lost my cool with the consultant, as I was adamant I wasn't going to lose my hair – Becky tried to calm me down, but losing my hair really touched a nerve with me.

I'll always remember telling my daughter Brooke the news later on. She hadn't batted an eyelid to any of my previous operations for numerous rugby injuries, but when I told her that I'd be having treatment to make me feel better and that I might lose my hair, she went upstairs and brought down a pink wig from her bedroom. Love her.

A week later, just before the start of the chemo treatment, they wanted to check that the scarring following my operation had sufficiently healed to start the chemo. A young nurse was given the task of checking the scarring, so I removed my trousers so she could examine me. Next thing I know, she'd whipped out her phone! I immediately reacted with shock – she could see by my reaction what I was thinking, and she apologised and explained that she was using the torch on her phone to have a better look. I thought my private parts were going to be all over social media! Fortunately, the scarring had healed enough for me to start my treatment, so my journey to beat cancer was about to begin.

It was decided that I'd have the BEP treatment, which is named after the initials of the drugs used: bleomycin, etoposide and cisplatin, which is a platinum compound. How it was administered for me was via a cannula, a short, thin tube which is put into a vein in your arm. The three drugs are given to you separately as drips into the cannula and are administered via a pump which releases the drugs over a set period. With cisplatin, additional fluids are administered to prevent damage to your kidneys. When you start the treatment, having the injections and lines put in that will pass the chemo around your body via your veins is nothing short of terrifying. Before you have the chemo, fluids are passed around your body just to flush any impurities out of your veins. The chemo's brought in reinforced black safety bags and the people carrying them are wearing big protective gloves – at the end of the day, the medication's poisonous, as it's trying to kill off the disease.

Velindre were superb. I had a room to myself throughout my stay, which I really appreciated as I'm a very private person. That first day I was really ill after the chemo. After a few days, though, once the medical staff had adapted the anti-sickness medication to fit my needs, the sickness initially wore off. I remember in the early days of the treatment saying to one of my nurses, 'This chemo isn't so bad.' She just gave me a look as if to say, 'There's worse to come', and of course she was right. I remember one of the nurses telling me, early on in my treatment when we were having a general conversation about chemo and cancer, that some people just can't cope with the required treatment. She told me about a man who came to them with cancer and after having the first lot of treatment, just never came back as he couldn't cope with it. Even now, I still wonder what happened to him, and what his limited life must have been like. Pretty sobering stuff.

The process was that five litres of chemo a day would go through your body in five-day cycles. A bag of chemo, which is one litre in size, takes one hour to get into your system and then a bag of saline would take thirty minutes. I looked forward to the saline, as that part meant you were almost at the end of that particular treatment for that day. The chemo treatment was divided into what was called cycles. Each cycle would take three to four weeks, with regular tests and constant checking of my blood markers/white blood cells, and with a rest period after each cycle. To be able to start a new cycle, the white blood cells have to be at a certain level – if it's too low, then it's too dangerous to continue until there's an improvement.

When you were having the chemo you could move around if you needed to go to the toilet, the intravenous drip attached to you and the bag hooked up on a stand which you could wheel along. Although Velindre always provided a meal, I never felt full due to the treatment I was on, so Becky always made me a packed lunch as well when I was in for the day having treatment. Very often I was just sitting on the bed tucking into food whilst liquids passed around my body!

During the second cycle of chemo I was asked to be a guest on the BBC for the Wales vs Australia game in the Autumn Series. One of my biggest fears when going through the chemo, as mentioned before, was losing my hair, which I'm sure is an issue for other chemo patients. A few days prior to being on the television, I felt that my hair was getting a lot thinner – what I didn't know then was that Becky was finding more and more hairs on my pillow in bed, but as she knew my feelings on losing my hair, she was hiding the evidence from me. I do know, though, that on the day of the game, I didn't wash my hair in case I lost even more before the BBC broadcast.

I went on the television and felt it went well, and got some kind comments from people about how I was looking and that it was good to see me back on TV, etc., which was nice. After discussing it with Becky, I decided to contact my hairdresser, Karen, and ask her to come over and shave my hair off. One of my friends, Scott, and my Uncle Dave also shaved their heads in support at the same time, which was a lovely gesture. After that, I used to wear a beanie whenever I went anywhere.

Apart from the really bad days, I trained throughout my treatment. I used to have to have a new cannula put in each time I visited to have chemo, as it came out each day so I could do weight training. Cardio work was out of the question – I did try to do some running with John Miles but after four 50-metre runs, I was on my knees gasping for air, as the drugs made me out of breath and my lungs wouldn't allow me to run. But in terms of weights, I could lift pretty close to what I'd been able to achieve prior to the treatment. Some people may find it crazy that I was continuing to train, but I needed something to occupy my mind. It almost felt like a few stolen hours of escape from my ongoing battle with cancer, and being able to train with Cardiff Blues and see the boys certainly lifted my spirits. It made me feel like one of the squad again having banter with people such as Bradley Davies and Lou Reed, who were constantly taking the mick – it felt like I was back to being a normal rugby player prior to having cancer.

The support I received from the nurses and doctors at Velindre during my time there was outstanding – I can't thank them enough. I built up a great rapport with them, and used to bring in profiteroles for them to share as a small way of saying thank you. The work they do for people in the horrible situations they find themselves in is nothing short of incredible, and they deserve so much credit. The Cardiff Blues, my friends and my family were all amazing: a huge thank you in particular to Becky, Ray, Scott and Uncle Dave, who were there throughout my treatment to keep my spirits up. I received messages from people around the rugby world, as well as messages from people I'd never met, wishing me well in my recovery. I'm so grateful to them all.

There were also events such as Cardiff Blues players shaving their heads in support and to raise money for Velindre. Cardiff Blues also sold wristbands in dark and light blue with the words 'Smile for your Captain', and many Cardiff Blues and rugby fans wore these around, which was very uplifting for my spirits and again raised a large amount of money for this amazing charity. Rhondda Schools U15s rugby team also shaved their heads in support and my Uncle Dave and friends completed a sponsored walk from Llanelli to Tonyrefail, taking in the grounds of the other rugby teams that I've played for – Llanelli Scarlets, Treorchy, Pontypridd and Cardiff Blues – along the route. All these events and more, too many to mention here, just show how great people can be and I'll never forget all the support I had. All I can say, from the heart, is thank you from me and my family.

Of course, doing the treatment there were some dark days when I had no energy and just felt terrible. The cocktail of drugs I had did come with side effects, including hearing loss, damaged taste buds and numbness in your fingers, as well as the aforementioned hair loss and sickness. I was impacted by them all on some level. During the darkest days I remained positive in front of the family, especially Becky and Brooke, but when alone, I'm not ashamed to say I felt very down.

On Christmas Day 2013 I was having chemo, which changed my Christmas routine. I went in for chemo early so I could have Christmas dinner at home with the family, and I remember vividly that over the New Year I was really ill. I was bedridden for a few days – those were probably the worst days of treatment I had. But I was determined to get through it and beat this. I couldn't leave my wife and daughter on their own in this world without me by their side. I was going to be a survivor of cancer.

In January 2014 after those initial bad days, I started to feel a lot better, and test results were bringing back some really positive results. My red and white blood cell markers were greatly improved and shortly afterwards I was given the news I'd longed to hear: I was given the all-clear. When you're told that your body's free of cancer, you still have regular checks to ensure it hasn't returned. In the first year you have checks every three months; in the second year, every six months; and then after that, a check every five years. Waiting for those results is stressful, but luckily you don't have too long to wait and thankfully, all of my results have been cancer-free. To celebrate overcoming cancer, Becky, Brooke and I went to Tenerife for the week, to spend time as a family and to be thankful for what we'd overcome.

When I got back, I started training full-time. I was training as hard as I could, with Bradley Davies and Dan Baugh giving their own time to do extra sessions with me starting at 6 a.m., to help me regain the fitness I needed to make a full return to rugby. In mid-February, Cardiff Blues released a press statement confirming I'd been given the all-clear and was back in training, and the reaction I got from everyone was so positive. I had to return to playing at the top level again to show people you can overcome adversity if you put your mind to it, and with some fortune on your side then anything's possible.

On 29th March 2014, I did indeed return to playing, coming off the bench after 57 minutes in a victory over Ulster at Cardiff Arms Park. The reception I got from Cardiff Blues and Ulster fans when I came onto the pitch and the stadium announcer said my name will remain with me forever. It was a very emotional time for me and for my family. I was back playing the game I loved, something I could only dream about only just over five months before when I was diagnosed. I managed to get in a few games at the end of that season. At the end of May, there was a Welsh trial game where Gats selected two sides to play each other called the Probables and the Possibles, for players to try to gain a place on the upcoming summer tour to South Africa. I was selected for the Possibles and we ended up on the wrong end of a 55 points to 7 scoreline. However, I was named that evening in the Welsh squad to tour South Africa, due to my form playing for Cardiff Blues after returning from illness. I ended up playing in two Tests, including the second Test that we should have won – which would have been an amazing, because at the time of writing, that's my last game in a Wales shirt. 61 caps won, and as it stands, the most-capped Wales hooker of all time, which I'm immensely proud about. Playing two games for my country after beating cancer is an achievement I'm very proud of, and who knows – I'm still playing, so I could still gain more caps (highly doubtful, but I'm only a phone call away, Gats)!

CHAPTER 15

The Best of...

SOMETHING I THOUGHT might be a bit different would be to look back over my career and answer some questions that readers may find my views of interest on. I've also included my Greatest Wales XV by position, drawn from players who were outstanding during my years playing for my country. I hope you enjoy it.

1. Best hooker I've ever played against?
It would be one of three: Mario Ledesma of Argentina, Keven Mealamu of New Zealand or Raphaël Ibañez of France. I'm going with Ledesma, one of the best scrummaging hookers I've ever faced and very well respected by all – and a main reason why Argentina became a real force in international rugby.

2. Best player ever played with?
I'm going for Regan King of the Scarlets. So much time on the ball, and made other players around him look special with the space he created. Unfortunate to only win just the one cap for New Zealand, but that shows just how good the All Blacks are. If he had not left New Zealand when he did, I'm certain he could easily have won a lot more caps for them.

3. Best player ever played against?
Richie McCaw of New Zealand. I played against him on a few occasions. One of the greatest players ever – all those caps for New Zealand, and he was regularly pinpointed by opponents as the player to target. He did at times get away with things that others couldn't – pushing the boundaries of the offside line, etc. But what a player.

4. Toughest player ever played with or against?

Richie McCaw again. Took so many hidings but just carried on playing. I'll always remember Andy Powell giving him a cheap shot when Wales played New Zealand in Cardiff – McCaw was pretty much knocked out cold, but got up and just got on with the game with no mention to the ref about what had happened. 148 appearances for New Zealand in his career just show his endurance and longevity in the game at the very highest level. McCaw was such a threat and such a key player for both the Crusaders and New Zealand that the opposition used to specifically target him – despite that, he still had a huge impact on all the games he played, showing the calibre of the player.

5. Best stadium played at?

Newlands, Cape Town just edges it over the Principality Stadium. I've played there only once, for the British Lions against Western Province in 2009. It's an old-school one, a historic South African stadium with a great atmosphere generated in the ground.

6. Best match played in?

A tough one. The Triple Crown game at Croke Park in 2008 and the second Test in 2009 for the British Lions against South Africa were both great games, but the best for me was winning my 50th cap for Wales against France for the Grand Slam in 2012. A huge moment, winning 50 caps in Cardiff and also winning the Grand Slam.

7. Best coach I've been coached by?

I'm going for Gats, based on the success he's had with the many teams he's managed and how he helped adapt my own game. He manages games and players so well, making the right calls at crucial times. A close second is Shaun Edwards, another fantastic coach and a born winner. Another coach who deserves a mention is Matt Sherratt, who did a great job at Cardiff Blues and no doubt will at the Ospreys.

8. Favourite country visited in a rugby capacity?

My choice for this is New Zealand, which I toured once with Wales. I'm choosing it for its history and tradition and for being the number one country in World Rugby for so many years. The passion for rugby in the country's very impressive and great to be around.

9. The best team I've played in?

I've been very fortunate through my career to play in some very good sides. The British and Irish Lions in 2009 were excellent and the 2006–07 Scarlets were also a fine side, but my choice is the Wales team of 2008. We won the Grand Slam with players such as Shane Williams, Mike Phillips, Lee Byrne, Stephen Jones, Adam Jones, Gethin Jenkins and Martyn Williams, just to name a few. We played great rugby along the way and it was a fabulous side to play in.

Smiler's Greatest Wales XV

15. Gareth Thomas – It was a close call between Alfie and Lee Byrne, but I just couldn't leave Alfie out of the team. A huge presence on the rugby field for Wales.

14. George North – When he burst onto the scene as a teenager, you knew he was going to be a special talent. Immensely strong and a great finisher.

13. Jonathan Davies – Tom Shanklin was close to selection, but Foxy's an outstanding centre in defence and attack, and has shown on Lions tours just how good a player he is against the very best. When I first met him, in Foxy's first pre-season at the Scarlets, I thought he was a hooker from his build. In one of the first sessions, Foxy lined up with the forwards I was up against, and I asked him what position he played as I thought he might be a threat to my position – I was amazed when the response was 'centre'.

12. Scott Williams – Have selected Scott over Jamie Roberts, who's been fantastic for Wales, for his all-round game. Scott can carry the ball into contact but also has the ability to move it wide, to see space behind defences and to put through different types of kicks. He has a very physical edge to his game – a much underrated player.

11. Shane Williams – Simply has to be in my team. Scored tries for Wales out of nothing with his huge talent on a rugby field. A fantastic player.

10. Stephen Jones – A general on a rugby field, a huge competitor who always gave his all. As with Scott, I don't feel he always gets the credit for how good a player he was.

9. Dwayne Peel – Peely gets the nod over Mike Phillips – both excellent players but I just feel that Peely offered you a bit more speed and tempo than Mike, which I'm looking for in my side.

1. Gethin Jenkins – Iestyn Thomas deserves a mention as one of the best scrummaging props I've ever played with, but I had to select Melon. Without a doubt, one of the most consistent players over the years for Wales. Probably not up there with the best loose heads for scrummaging, but he has more than made up for it with his work rate around the field. He's achieved so much in the game, and if I hadn't selected him, I couldn't put up with his moaning at me.

2. Matthew Rees – It's my greatest Wales XV, so I'm picking myself!

3. Adam Jones – Bomb was one of the best tight heads in the world in his prime, especially at scrummaging, which is the most important skill in this position. He was the cornerstone for Wales for a number of years. Has to be my starting 3.

4. Bradley Davies – Someone who thinks he is a full-time body builder and part-time rugby player – he loves the gym! In saying that, I have a lot of respect for Brad. A tough opponent and never gives in. Enjoys the nitty gritty side of the game, and has a big physical presence. It was close between Brad and Luke Charteris, but am going with Brad over Charts for his all-round game.

5. Alun Wyn Jones – A total no brainer, this selection. This guy trains as he plays, with so much energy and commitment. Played his first game for Wales at 6, but soon moved to his preferred position in the boiler house. AWJ is one of the greatest second rows Wales has ever produced – a great leader on and off the field. He'd be my captain every game.

6. Dafydd Jones – Was forced to retire from rugby with a shoulder injury, unfortunately. I enjoyed playing with Daf, a true warrior. Could do all you wanted as a 6. Always a great line-out option, more often than not at the tail, he had a big physical presence in defence and attack. He won 42 caps for Wales, and would have won a lot more but for a number of injuries through his career.

7. Martyn Williams – I had to think hard about this one. Do I choose Nugget or Sam Warburton? It was a close one, but I'm going with Nugget. Nugget wasn't the most physical or strongest openside that I've played with, and he would be the first to admit that, but his rugby ability was impressive and he always seemed to be in the right place at the right time. When he had the ball, his decision making and ability to spot an attacking opportunity were second to none. Both Nugget and Warbs were brilliant at the ruck, but I'm just going with Nugget.

8. Taulupe Faletau – Tough one to pick with Ryan Jones and Alix Popham, who I've been fortunate to play with as well, also in the running. But it would have to be Taulupe Faletau. I remember when Taulupe was first selected in the Welsh squad. He was very quiet and shy, but he's got a skill set that you could only dream of. Has achieved so much in the game at such a young age.

It's been an honour to take to the field with these players and the others I played with over my career. Thanks for all the amazing memories.